THE GREAT AMERICAN SWAPATHON IS ON!

All over the country, people are trading goods, services and skills, using less money, conserving energy and recycling materials. You can be part of it!

Back to Barter Shows You . . .

how to organize individual trades, how to get involved in non-profit barter co-ops and skills exchanges.
Other sections take you through profit-oriented barter networks and real estate trading.

How to Save on Taxes . . .

A special chapter on barter taxes brings you up to date on areas of IRS interest.

How to Find a Barter Partner . . .

Check the final section and find out what non-profit barter groups are working—and where. You'll also discover information on general and for-profit barter groups, publications, vacation exchanges.

Have Fun, Use Your Creativity, Meet New People—and *Save Money* on Your Way . . .

BACK TO BARTER!

BACK TO BARTER

What'll You Take For It?

ANNIE PROULX

PUBLISHED BY POCKET BOOKS NEW YORK

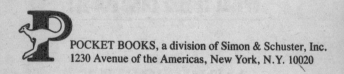

P POCKET BOOKS, a division of Simon & Schuster, Inc.
1230 Avenue of the Americas, New York, N.Y. 10020

. . . for my mother

". . . wealth, education, research and many other things are needed for any civilisation, but what is most needed today is a revision of the ends which these means are meant to serve. And this implies, above all else, the development of a life-style which accords to material things their proper, legitimate place, which is secondary and not primary."

E. F. SCHUMACHER

Contents

Foreword

A.W. Gorton ran the Combination Cash Store in Manchester Center, Vermont, for a many profitable year.

He dickered, traded, even wagered, and otherwise accumulated wealth at a time when making money in a country grocery store depended on skillful bartering. Farmers and their families came to town, not to "buy groceries" or to "shop," but to "trade," and they meant exactly that. They brought in eggs and chickens, meats of all kinds, maple syrup, apples, and garden produce, to trade for staples.

A.W. was always ready to make a deal with a customer, and you didn't need something to trade to join in the fun. If you bought cheese off the big wheel under the glass dome, he'd knife off a taste for you, a generous sample for himself, then offer you double-or-nothing that he could cut a slice within one ounce of what you wanted, and you name the amount. He'd be right on the mark on the simple order of one pound, and I never saw him give away cheese when the customer tried to mix him up with an order for something like 19¾ ounces. I don't know yet whether he had a good eye or an educatd thumb on the scales.

A.W. was a good teacher for this clerk-sweeper-stocker-of-shelves. He taught by example.

Ira Edgarton came in from Rupert. "I've got a couple crates of strawberries out in the truck," he told A.W. "Like you to take them and put them toward what I owe you."

It was a common practice for A.W. to carry his customers. They would pay him when they could, with cash or goods.

A.W. and Ira looked over the strawberries, then they dickered for a few minutes, with A.W. explaining how hard times were, with people not paying their bills, not even buying much. A.W. said he was sure he'd lose money on the strawberries, but he'd take them off Ira's hands—at the right price. Ira finally gave in at ten cents a quart for the ninety-six quarts.

This meant A.W. credited Ira's account at the store for $9.60. Only of course the groceries on Ira's bill hadn't cost A.W. that amount. Let's say A.W. got the strawberries for about $7.00 in money out of his pocket.

Ira unloaded the strawberries in the back entrance leading into the cellar. A.W. called me downstairs, suggested I get some extra strawberry boxes out of the storeroom, then sat me down on a small stool beside the crates.

"Now pour," he ordered.

"Pour?"

"That's right. Pour. Take one box of strawberries and pour it into that empty box. Fill it right up— heaping. Do the same with all those boxes."

It sounded like a waste of time, but it was his dollar a day, and it was cool and comfortable down there. I poured.

And then the magic struck me. I was doing just as he told me to, filling the boxes high, but each time there would be a few berries left over in the first box. The berries had been packed tightly when picked. By pouring, I was letting a lot of air into each basket. And when I had poured the ninety-six, I had 106 quarts, plus a handful or maybe two for eating.

By the time I had carried them upstairs, A.W. had a big sign, "STRAWBERRIES, 15¢," outside. By midafternoon we were out of strawberries; there was $15.90 (that's more than 100 percent profit) additional in the cash register; and A.W. had a lot of satisfied customers, people like Jennie Stone and Anna Harwood who bought strawberries and complimented A.W. for filling those baskets so high and thus giving the customers something extra.

A.W. liked a trade like that, where everybody went away happy—and there was something extra in his pocket.

He would have liked Annie Proulx's book. She, like him, recognizes that there's much more to barter than mere profit.

There's that chance to get rid of something that's cluttering up the house and get something you need, and know the warm glow that comes with consummation of a good trade—and the sharp sting when you suddenly know that you've been "took."

There's the chance to do something for someone, and to have someone do something for you in return, and who is to say which offers the greater satisfaction? And there's the possibility of making friends with people willing to trade not only possessions and work, but recipes, information, and ideas. You can even temporarily exchange homes, as you'll read in this book.

Here's a book for city-dwellers as well as country folk. It acknowledges that each one of us cannot be self-sustaining. It suggests a satisfying and profitable arrangement for exchanging our possessions and our skills to the benefit of all.

We'll agree with Annie, and we expect that Robert Frost would as well, that "Good swaps make good neighbors." Read this book and you'll understand why.

MARC ROGERS

CHAPTER 1

Why Barter?

This is a different kind of how-to book, concerned with the practical art of living a rich and deeply satisfying life with little cash and credit, through practicing traditional barter skills and attitudes.

Barter will not replace a cash income, but can liberally supplement it, improve your relations with your neighbors, conserve energy, recycle goods, and help homesteaders and small-scale farmers bridge the chasm between poverty and comfort by providing a market for minor produce. For many, barter means the difference between sleepless nights worrying about money, and the sense of security that goes with knowing your own skills and products will supply many of life's necessaries and pleasures so that the limited cash can go for "money only" things—gas, taxes, telephone, electricity. This technique of trading *around* your cash money leads to a freedom from total wage dependence that few people know.

Barter is the grease that makes the rural wheels go around.

The Rural Renaissance

For decades people have been leaving the cities and suburbs for the countryside. Between 1970 and 1976 small towns and rural communities grew by 4.3 million people, and the trend continues. This exodus has taken two forms—the outer ring of settlement beyond the suburbs into countrified surroundings, and the shift to the rural hinterlands where there are no nearby urban areas. So far outward have these exurban rings spread that the 288 metropolitan areas in the United States now cover one-fifth of the total land surface of this country.

Some people move from the cities and suburbs to escape taxes and crime, traffic and pollution. Countless others find something lacking in a life spent producing and accumulating goods and gadgets, judging your worth by the denominators of money, possessions, and credit lines. Some, troubled by the negative tendency of industry and our civilization to use up the earth's irreplaceable resources, decide to try for a more truly productive life on the land that will provide many of their own needs and generate a modest income through labor-intensive, organic methods. Some

are lured by the security of independence of farm life. A few are attracted by a vague sense of "country chic." To them rural life means little beyond wearing work clothes and burning wood. Others have moved backwoods out of a pervasive sense of malaise, abandoning unsatisfying jobs and set hours of "leisure" (usually spent watching a television set) in the belief that forty hours a week of boring, salaried tasks which have little relation to real physical *work* have damaged their capacities for imaginative innovation in their own lives. They rebel against the silent dictum that their major creative outlet is to purchase or charge goods.

Some people go back to the land with a comfortable bankroll, some with a little money and a solid background in rural farm living, but too many go with neither experience of country life nor the substantial savings that will support them while they learn. For this last group rural living can be a bitter and costly experience if they approach country life with city values and expectations.

The New Small Farms

People coming onto the land are settling on small farms of fifty acres, homesteads of five acres, and in small rural villages. The goal of most of these millions is to own or occupy land, for they instinctively understand that the amount of land is finite, that the land is the source of life, and that it is steadily disappearing under asphalt and concrete.

Yesterday's farms are today's factories, shopping centers, sewage treatment plants, subdivisions, parking lots, and, above all, highways. The best farmland—the flat, rich soils along the major waterways and in the fertile valleys—is unfortunately the easiest and cheapest to develop.

Most of these small homesteads and new farms are the carved-up remains of the big farms of the nineteenth and early twentieth centuries, farms of 400 and 500 acres, with hay meadows, pastureland, wood-lots, sugar bush, farm ponds, and cropland. Very few of the new small parcels of land have the diversity of natural resources or range of terrain types to supply a true farm's needs. Instead, one family will buy the pasturelands, another the old woodlot, still another buyer will get the hayfields and the spring, and perhaps several new settlers will have the flat cropland.

For any of these homesteads to be successful, a natural barter economy on a very local scale is neces-sary. The family with the pastureland needs hay and corn for winter stock feed, so they may swap some pastureland rights with the hayfield-owning neighbor and the cropland neighbor, neither of whom has pas-ture. They all barter—fresh milk, butter, beef, mulch hay for the garden—with the family that owns the woodlot, to get fence posts, firewood, and building timber. Only through barter can the efficiency and local self-containment of the large old farm be re-stored.

Some Thrive, Some Survive, Some Leave

In the past few years the USDA has been giving greater attention to the family farm and the small-scale farmer; first, by revising the definition of a "small farm"; second, through the publication of the 1978 Yearbook of Agriculture, *Living on a Few Acres;* and by starting a six-year pilot program of founding and funding new family farms with very small acreage in the South, a program in which low-income farmers will get needed training and a chance to buy land.

The new definition of a "small farm" is a radical departure from the old dictum that any farm that grossed less than $20,000 annually in sales was "small" and played little part in the national economy, a definition and an attitude that alienated the USDA from hundreds of thousands of hardworking, struggling farm people. The new approach, which comes up with the startling information that 38 percent of American farm families live and work on *small farms,* has three criteria: that the farm family provides most of the labor and management of the farm; that total farm income from all sources is below the median nonmetropolitan family income in the state; that the farm family depends on farming for a significant portion of its income. "Significant" means at least 10 percent of the family income earned through farming.

One of the crucial problems of the small farmer is finding a local market for what he produces, for the small farmer cannot compete with the big fellows in bulk shipping to urban markets. Yet many so-called

"But we ate 10 percent of our own zucchini!"

"agricultural states," like Vermont, import 85 percent and more of their food from the West and the South while local small-scale stock, truck, and fruit farmers anxiously worry about where to sell their products. The market is there—locally—but it has to be developed. A good beginning point is through barter and area farmers' markets where trading for both cash and goods is lively.

WOOD, GRAIN, etc.
Persons who have contracted to Pay for Papers, Books, &c. in WOOD are informed that the time for delivering the same will be extended to the 15th of February next. Those wishing to pay in Grain, Hay, or other articles of produce are requested to bring it in immediately.

Vermont Republican & Journal, Jan. 7, 1832

Success Stories

Despite an initial lack of practical knowledge and limited cash markets, many homesteaders and small-scale farmers are making successes of their new lives. Some have built their own houses with timber from their land, started small truck-farm operations, raised pigs for a community market, bred sheep for wool and seasonal lamb markets, raised chickens for egg and broiler sales, rabbits, bees, Christmas trees, dairy goats, earthworms, Thanksgiving turkeys; some have baked homemade bread, some made maple syrup for taxes and trading, some have started garden plant nurseries in small, self-built greenhouses; some have learned or practice crafts such as chair-caning, basketry, weaving, sewing, quilting, and decoy carving. Some are raising minks for the fur trade, and some are raising herbs that they dry and sell through mail order. Some have started seed companies and bicycle repair

shops, some make furniture, and some make hay. For many country people these are full-time occupations, for some they supplement a paycheck.

These people are succeeding, not only through hard work, imagination, and stamina, but because they have developed a feeling for the cooperative economic process that keeps rural farm communities and their inhabitants lively and thriving—the bartering, trading, and swapping of everything from surplus produce to labor, goods, machinery, and equipment, skills, services, ideas, instruction, and knowledge among each other. Some newcomers learn quickly, like Karla Milovich of Little Valley, New York.

When my husband and I moved to the country a short five years ago, I doubt that we truly realized what an education we were in store for. One of the very first things we learned when our move was still in the wishing and hoping stages was the great art of the swap or trade. . . . We have since, many times grown a friendship with a little down home trading. We barter eggs for fresh milk, home canned pickles, or home baked bread for cream to make butter. But the best swap we have formulated is something we worked out with some dear and close friends. We call it "work parties. . . ." The work has ranged from putting in a foundation for a greenhouse, to cutting wood, to fixing our old pickup. At butchering time we all pitch in. We all bring something and swap some good recipes, homesteading tips and fellowship round the stove.

Letters to the Editor,
Farmstead, No. 31, Summer, 1980

Many of the new rural folks are not able to adapt to country ways. Some cannot break the lifetime habit of

buying everything they need in a store. Others don't recognize the myth of independent subsistence farming as unrealistic, and struggle along trying the almost impossible task of raising, making, or producing everything the family needs on their homesteads. They have no thought of producing a surplus crop, stock, or specialty craft, or of developing a skill needed in the community that they could barter for the needed items they find difficult or impossible to produce themselves. For these people who either continue to depend on cash income and store purchases, or who vainly try to supply all their needs on the homestead themselves, rural life often turns into discouraging, unremitting labor with no time to enjoy the fruits of life or the land. Some end by clasping the cold hand of rural poverty, and after a while they give up and return to the nine-to-five grind in the city, or practice the tedious Country Commute over long distances between the homestead and a job.

Yet some enterprising swappers can turn even this situation to their advantage. Don Weseman of De Soto, Missouri, says:

> Although we've made our move to the country, it's still necessary for me to maintain my city job . . . and a lot of our bartering is done with our urban friends. [One] makes wine from the apples, peaches, blackberries and strawberries we bring him in return for half the finished product.
>
> Last winter I delivered a cord of firewood to a city dweller in exchange for some much-needed electrical work on our house.

Swapping fresh country produce with city friends and clientele can pay for the expense and nuisance of commuting. Part of bartering is developing the imagination to turn a negative situation into an advantage through a swap.

Country Barter

Barter, one of the most stable economic systems because it deals with real needs and real values, is enjoying a surge of popularity in the face of fluctuating currency values, wavering faith in the soundness of the dollar, double-digit inflation, rising unemployment, tightening credit, and sky-high interest rates as well as the fear that recession could turn into depression.

☞ Trade exchange clubs with branches in major cities from coast to coast are proliferating. Some of these clubs are sophisticated businesses that use computers and credit cards, and mail out monthly statements to their members. More than 250 of these exchange organizations exist today; most of them are California-based.

☞ Countless local barter organizations in small towns, cities, major metropolitan areas, and retirement communities are staffed by swap-minded members who

help people make contact with each other to trade
local transportation, small repair services, tutoring,
baby-sitting, dog-walking, and hundreds of domestic
chores and jobs.

☞ Newspapers, "shoppers'" magazines, radio stations, supermarket bulletin boards, and the front doors
of general stores increasingly carry "swap" notices
and columns. *Yankee* magazine's barter columns date
back to the publication's beginnings. (Legend has it
that the magazine itself was started through Robb
Sagendorph's "swap" for a half-interest in a print
shop.) A rural paper published in Jupiter, Florida, *The
Country Journal,* offers a free listing in its swap column to subscribers, and for several years *Mother
Earth News* has been trading free subscriptions for
letters describing successful barter experiences.

☞ Swap boxes are everywhere, in front of stores, ga-
rages, co-ops—wherever people gather or pass.

☞ Swap festivals and barter fairs are drawing increasing numbers of eager barterers. Some of them attract
thousands of people and last for several days.

☞ Church and senior citizens' groups have started
barter clubs and organizations not only for needed services and goods, but to add vigor, interest, and pride
to too-quiet lives.

☞ Sovereign nations swap on a grand scale—wheat,
munitions, tractors, planes, and oil.

☞Big business, both international and national, trades
surplus stocks of everything from pig iron to panty
hose, and barters advertising, travel, and hotel accommodations for goods and credits in complicated three-
and four-way deals.

"Aw, come on!"

On the local level, every day there are hundreds of thousands of simple, basic, one-to-one plain swaps between two willing barterers. Nowhere is barter more natural, more suitable, and more efficient than in rural areas, small towns, and communities. In farm country barter has never stopped.

Aside from getting something you need or want in exchange for something you have too much of, or don't need any more, barter has a dozen positive side benefits.

Barter cuts across class, ethnic, age, and income-level categories like a hot knife through butter.

Barter helps children and adults recognize their *real* personal worth and ability, not through bank accounts, paychecks, or brand-name possessions, but through the actual abilities they have to *do* or *make* something, *grow* something, or *raise* something. Barterers take pride in their work and skills.

Barter creates a community of interests, puts wasted or neglected talents to use, including those of children and the elderly who are usually on the fringes of economic action in a cash and credit system because their ability to earn a wage is nil.

Barter makes good neighbors. Alice and Don Hooper of Brookfield, Vermont, have a herd of thirty-eight dairy goats, and sell their milk to New England health-food stores. They do not own much farm machinery, but have worked out a satisfying swap with a good neighbor; in return for the use of his tractor and mowing and baling machinery, the Hoopers give him hay as well as their labor at haying time.

In Gig Harbor, Washington, the Diedrich family knows that good swaps make good neighbors:

> Since moving to the country, we've established "trade relations" with three different families. In each case the friendship that's blossomed is a result of the swap that originally got us acquainted.

Their trades ran from rotating transport for preschool children to teaching a neighbor how to raise and race sled dogs in exchange for his help with their own team, to a swap of young raspberry plants for cucumber sets.

Another family in Renton, Washington, went back to the land on a tight budget, but rapidly caught on to the advantages of bartering. One neighbor swapped the use of his tractor and blade so they could level their building site, in return for the hay from their four-acre field; another neighbor dug a mile of waterline trenches for them with his backhoe in swap for cattle-grazing rights on their unused pasture; then, after they graded the driveway, they swapped excess topsoil for a job of carpet installation. With satisfaction they say, "The swaps go on and on." So do the examples of good swapping neighbors.

Barter recycles goods, clothing, and materials that are too often just tossed out in our throw-away society. Children's clothing, grown out but not worn out, is an obvious trade, but a handy, repair-minded soul can take in broken windows and dead toasters, sputtering lawn mowers, armless rocking chairs, zipperless blue jeans, faltering houseplants, untrained dogs, malfunctioning trucks, unraveled sweaters, ax heads without handles, and a thousand other trash-barrel candidates and fix them up again with a little tinkering, remedial labor, and patience.

A Connecticut barterer with a sharp trader's eye noticed that an "astounding" number of slightly worn or barely damaged garden hoses and lawn chairs were tossed away at the end of the summer by the residents of his town. He collects these discards from sidewalk trash pickup points, takes them home, then repairs the chairs with new webbing and splices the hoses with hose-connectors he gets at close-out sales. He swaps the refurbished hoses and chairs, still with plenty of life left in them, for things he needs at the beginning of

the next summer when his hoses and chairs are in demand, and comments:

> When I barter, my greatest joy isn't saving money
> . . . but in utilizing something someone else has
> given up on, or preventing *my* castoffs from be-
> coming landfill.

Barter within a community is energy-efficient, and cuts down on the fuel-gobbling runs to distant towns and shopping centers. A Michigan study comparing the energy uses of urban and rural families concluded that although energy use in the home was about the same, rural families used 42 percent more gasoline than their urban counterparts. As gasoline and fuel oil costs rise and rise, country people will have to think how they can get what they need close to home. Swapping the output from your ice-cream freezer for a piece of copper pipe to finish your plumbing project makes more sense than driving twenty miles to the nearest plumbing supply store while your neighbor goes twelve miles for some inferior, store-bought ice cream.

Barter is entertaining and even exciting. It vigorously exercises your ingenuity and gives you the satisfying feeling of thrift and efficiency that comes with the conclusion of a successful trade. The happiest barterers are those who find a lifelong "trading partner"—neighbor, relative or friend. Rural trading partners swap everything—labor, help, transportation, produce, barn-sitting, seed potatoes, and a pull out of the ditch—comfortably and as a matter of course. They don't keep an account of who owes what because it all evens out over the years. Some of these swap partnerships between rural families continue for generations.

Barter deals are never forgotten. Who knows where their money goes? Who can remember how they got the money they exchanged for a table radio back in 1938? But what you swap—labor or goods—for something sticks in your mind forever.

The Myth of Self-Sufficiency

It's a schoolroom belief that our colonial and pioneer ancestors were rugged individualists who strode out alone into the wilderness and hacked isolated farmsteads from the virgin forest with their axes, then provided themselves with all the complex necessities of life solely by the grinding labor of their

———◆•◦•◆———

Cowdry & Dutton of Phelp's Row. Cabinet and Chair Makers. WANTED, in exchange for their work, most kinds of LUMBER, such as Birch, Maple, Pine and Hemlock Scantling; Birch, Pine and Hemlock, (inch and half inch) Boards; Pine and Hemlock Planks—Also, Produce of all kinds, and a few cords of Fire Wood.

Vermont Republican & Journal, Nov. 8, 1833

own and their family's hands. Consider what was
needed: a house and a barn; a springhouse for water;
candles for light; a decent diet from garden, grains,
livestock, hunting and fishing; clothing, through the
dozens of tiresome and difficult steps from the flax
field and the sheep's back to the finished garment;
cleared and fenced pastures; plowed and harrowed
fields; an orchard, set out, pruned, and harvested;
bridges and traversable roads; sheep, cows, and goats
bred, milked, tended, and butchered; butter and
cheeses from the dairy house; cords and cords of
firewood for the profligate fireplaces; the harvest and
storage of hay, grains, fruits, vegetables; nails and
horseshoes, shovels and tools from the home forge;
wooden buckets and barrels, spoons, trenchers, and a
thousand other necessaries. A little reflection tells us
that just to cut, stack, haul, and split the twenty cords
of firewood the average early American home burned
every year took weeks and weeks of steady labor.

Yet some modern homesteaders have aimed at this
awesome picture of self-sufficiency as an ideal goal
without realizing it is not only unattainable, but never
existed. Probably the most successful attempts at self-
sufficiency and farm production of the necessities of
life were on the plantations of Rhode Island and Connecticut, and later the South, where slave labor made
such a goal possible. Only through communal efforts,
exchanging work and swapping and trading surplus
goods and skills, were the colonists able to provide for
themselves and, eventually, over several generations,
to build up thriving homesteads.

Modern homesteaders eventually recognize the im-
possibility of doing it all alone. A Washington State
couple says:

Three years ago we made the "big move" from
city to country living. At first we tried to handle
all the chores and "fix-ups" ourselves—both to

save money and to acquire some badly needed skills—but now we realize that we'll just *never* be able to do some jobs as well (or as efficiently) as a better-trained person. Still . . . how do you afford help when the engine won't run or the sewing gets too complicated? Barter, that's how!

Isolated, scattered farms were very unusual in colonial days. Only in the eighteenth century after several generations of hard work did outlying homesteads become common. In the early days houses were set up close together in villages with the inhabitants sharing common fields for grazing, common woods for firewood, and a common herdsman whose care of the stock animals gave others the time to pursue trades and avocations in addition to the necessary tillage of the soil. Few of the early settlers were experienced or full-time farmers except through necessity; many of them had had little farming experience before their arrival in the New World, and a good many of them came from towns and cities, not rural farmsteads, before they crossed the ocean. In the port of Charlestown, by 1640 the skilled craftsmen included charcoal burners, collar makers, anchor smiths, tailors, coopers, glaziers, rope makers, and tile makers. Agricultural historian Howard S. Russell comments that such an artisan would

. . . live on what would now be called "a little place," dig a garden, plant a few fruit trees; perhaps keep a cow and a hog or two, maybe a cosset sheep, all the larger animals to join the herd or flock cared for by the village herdsman. [He] . . . might also cut his hay on the village meadow and bring in his firewood, building timber, and tool handles from the common woodland.

A Deep, Long Furrow, p. 76.

The Traditional Barter Economy

In those early days some crops and some products were raised and made specifically for trade, such as tobacco, hard cider, potash, and timber. All quickly became part of the lively stream of international trade with Spain, Portugal, the West Indies, and England. This brought hard currency into the seaport towns. In the more remote farm and rural communities there were no banks and no currency, except beaver skins in the Connecticut Valley and wampum on Long Island. In Rhode Island, tobacco was the medium of exchange, and in Plymouth Colony, the currency was corn. Affairs were conducted mostly through barter, both the direct one-to-one exchanges and more complex trades, with hundreds of examples preserved in old account books, letters, and journals.

In 1640 Zaccheus Gould of Salem traded as "rent" 400 bushels of rye, 300 of wheat, 200 of barley plus 8 oxen, 5 cows, 2 heifers, 4 calves, and 2 mares for the lease of 300 acres of land. In 1648 John Endecott swapped 500 young apple whips with William Trask for 200 acres of land. In 1662 a bushel of turnips was a fair swap for a cord of oak firewood in Newbury. Taxes were payable in grain; ministers and schoolteachers were paid in meat, firewood, corn, and wheat. So brisk and so common was barter that the General Courts of Massachusetts and Connecticut both set up inspectors to regulate the quality and measurement of the most frequently traded items— biscuits, pipestaves, fish, leather, hides, lumber, and casks.

———◆◆◆———

"If I had my life to live over again, I would elect to be a trader of goods rather than a student of science. I think barter is a noble thing."

Albert Einstein

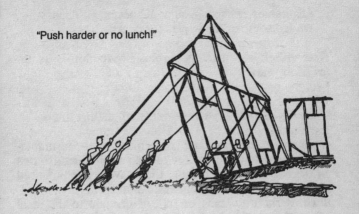

"Push harder or no lunch!"

On the more isolated farmsteads of the late eighteenth and early nineteenth centuries, it took the labor of the whole family just to provide the basic necessities of life as well as special products for barter use, such as bark for the tanneries, potash and pearlash for export, furs or charcoal or a dependable surplus of some sort, whether butter or eggs, stock, grain, fruits, timber, hides, or the handgoods of some cottage industry like woven hats, carded or hand-spun wool, or a hundred other manufactured items.

Successful rural families today still try to raise a surplus for barter. A couple of gardeners from Forks of Salmon, California, have a big garden and plenty of excess produce which they swap for what they don't have.

Last summer, for instance, we had a bumper crop of luscious raspberries so we traded some of the fruit for our neighboring friends' fresh eggs, raw milk, honey, and firewood. In the fall we needed apples, so a neighbor with a large orchard let us pick several crates in exchange for some of our vegetables, peaches, and peppermint. Then we traded some of the apples for pears.

The principle of trading surplus production is as ancient as man.

The Country Store—Missing Link

The extra produce and goods made by the farm family of the past were the key to their well-being, for this was their trading currency, their "swap goods," used often for one-to-one local swaps, taken to town or village markets to trade or sell, or brought to the local general store and bartered for shelf goods.

The rural store was the pivotal point of the farm barter economy of yesterday. Farm families brought in eggs, butter, cheese, poultry, and flaxseed which the storekeeper would look over and discuss with the customer. When a value was settled, the trade was made for credit, past bill due, or on-the-spot swap for specialty foods and all kinds of manufactured goods difficult to make at home—guns, traps, ammunition, spices, fashionable fabrics, enamel and tinware, china, molasses and sugar, jewelry, marbles, imported lemons, oranges, and bananas, coffee and tea, vanilla beans, clocks, harnesses, writing paper, books, patent medicines and salves, pocket knives, saws, mirrors and much, much more.

In the early nineteenth century locally produced silk floss was as good as gold at the country stores in the Connecticut Valley. In the autumn, just before the cattle buyer came around to the various stores, farmers would frequently settle up their accounts with fattened animals.

The storekeeper held the goods and livestock in storage—a henhouse for the chickens, a yard for the cattle, a cold springhouse for perishable eggs and butter—until the city merchants' buyers came around to collect farm produce which eventually went to urban consumers. The storekeeper got trade goods and cash, or whatever was agreeable and needed.

Some urban merchants set up their own exchange centers where they took in rural hams and cheeses in exchange for molasses, rum, plows, and rope. Cow traders regularly toured the general stores of the rural hinterlands swapping for hide cattle destined for the booming leather industry of Essex County, Massachusetts. The sharp horse traders, always on the lookout for a good swap—fast-talking and wise in the ways of horseflesh and men—used the storekeepers as contacts, for the storemen knew everybody and everybody's business, horses included.

Charles Morrow Wilson, author of *Let's Try Barter*, first published in 1960 and now something of an underground barter classic, first learned the value of a swap at a country store near Mount Comfort, Arkansas. He remarks that ". . . from 1890 to 1912, an average country store 'cleared' at least two-thirds of its annual trade in barter and where most rural families effected at least half of their living, such as it was, by direct barter."

He describes the typical farmer coming into Bill Plue's store with some eggs, a few gallons of molasses, a smoked ham, or some fresh sausage as a "down swap" on a pair of new overalls or a plow, and the farmer's wife "swappin' in" a few hens for some brown sugar or buttons. Every region had specialized swap items in addition to the standard eggs, butter, and chickens—in the South, home-dried goldenseal and ginseng root, wild walnuts, chestnuts, and hickory nuts; in the North, maple syrup, spruce gum, furs.

In 1933 there were an estimated 225,000 country stores in the United States, many of them still actively swapping. Today country stores are stocked with brand-name goods, canned vegetables, fast food items, and frozen foods, the same items found in big city and suburban stores. The storekeeper, who has to pay taxes, utility and telephone bills, and insurance, and deal with large national distributers, will take only cash or checks. No longer are rural stores, except for a small handful of holdouts in traditional bartering areas, meeting places for farm swappers.

Wendell Barry describes the situation in his powerful book, *The Unsettling of America*.

And nowhere now is there a market for minor produce; a bucket of cream, a hen, a few dozen eggs. One cannot sell milk from a few cows anymore; the law-required equipment is too expensive. Those markets were done away with in the name of sanitation—but, of course, to the enrichment of large producers. We have always had to have "a good reason" for doing away with small operators, and in modern times the good reason has often been sanitation, for which there is apparently no small or cheap technology. Future historians will no doubt remark upon the inevitable association, with us, between sanitation and filthy lucre. And it is one of the miracles of science and hygiene that the germs that used to be in our food have been replaced by poisons.

This "minor produce" that has no *cash* market, is the very lively medium of local barter. Thwarted by regulations and the disappearance of the trading country store, small-scale producers have created their own barter markets in many rural communities with their buckets of cream, fresh eggs, and plump hens.

Changing Work

One of the oldest and most effective forms of barter is swapping labor, or, as it was called in rural New England in the last century, "changing work." A family that needed help raising a barn, haying, threshing wheat, butchering, logging, land-clearing, stump-pulling, moving rock, building a fence, or a hundred other tasks where haste was imperative or the job impossible for a lone person, traded for their neighbor's labor with their own when it was needed. These cooperative exchanges still characterize life in rural communities where the links between humans, the soil, time, and the weather remain unbroken.

Merle Yoder of Tomah, Wisconsin, describes the back-and-forth rhythm of changing work:

Since we farm the old way—with horses—and put loose hay in the barn, it's easier if there's more than one doing the work. So my brother-in-law and I help each other with the hay. . . . We also cooperate when it comes to grain threshing and silo filling.

Jon Taylor in the Canadian province of Alberta, who swaps machinery and labor with a neighbor during haying time, says:

> . . . My neighbor and I keep our cooperative exchanges working throughout the year. Generally speaking, I do most of the jobs that require a mechanic, and he takes care of livestock problems. Most important though, is the fact that we both know help is available at any time of the night or day, without question or concern for repayment. . . . Virtually none of the farmers around here could afford to pay modern wages for as much help as we each now get by way of barter.

Depression Barter—Self-Help and Bootstrap Economics

Barter was familiar to most country people before the depression hit, especially in the Midwest where for years farm families had accepted aluminum tokens called "trade checks" in return for their produce. These tokens were good only at the store of issue. When the bank moratorium of March, 1933, brought the stumbling business procedures for the country to a full stop, there were already dozens of barter groups in operation. As the depression deepened, thousands of communities, towns, and cities looked to barter as the self-help solution to the moneyless, workless nightmare that had descended on the country and which government seemed powerless to cure. Some of the groups had grim names—The Unemployed Citizens' League of Seattle, and The Organized Unemployed of Minneapolis—and were strictly temporary arrangements. Others adopted a visionary ideal of a future moneyless society, and saw themselves as the vanguard of this utopian world.

So pervasive and widespread was barter that the U.S. Bureau of Labor Statistics did a detailed, nationwide survey of barter organizations during 1932, and in *The Monthly Labor Review* reported on hundreds of them, from The Ex-Servicemen's Nonpartisan Barter and Exchange Bureau, Inc., of Milwaukee, to The Citizens' Service Exchange of Richmond, Virginia. Hundreds of magazine and newspaper articles on the wildfire sweep of barter across the country appeared. Private citizens, farmers, big business, municipalities, church and charitable workers, social workers, all involved themselves in every possible variation of bartering from simple sharecropping to complex organizations with scrip, credits and debits, factories, and huge memberships.

One of the most successful barter experiments was the National Development Association of Salt Lake City, Utah, better known as the N.D.A. The group started in the fall of 1931 when there was a large number of unemployed workers in Salt Lake City, and a surplus of unharvested produce on outlying farms rotting in the fields because the farmers couldn't afford to hire the labor to pick the crops. Benjamin B. Stringham, a real estate man who owned a potato field, began trucking unemployed workers out to the farms

———◆—◗◗◗◗◗◗◆———

A FARM FOR SALE VERY, VERY CHEAP

The subscriber offers for sale, a good FARM, lying in the town of Plymouth, VT. eleven miles from Woodstock Court-House, containing about 100 acres, mostly under improvement, with two good Barns, Sheds, House, and well fenced.

Said farm will be sold extremely low for cash, grain, neat stock, pork, butter or cheese. A long pay day given if requested.   Geo. B. Green

Vermont Republican & Journal, June 21, 1833

daily, after they agreed to accept produce as pay. From this simple beginning the N.D.A. branched into six states with 30,000 members within a year.

Less than twelve months after Stringham drove the first bunch of men out to the farm area, the N.D.A. was operating two canning factories, a small oil refinery, a sawmill, a soap factory, a fruit-drying department, a tannery, a coal mine, and a sewing business. Its trade channels extended deep into the farmlands of the West and even into the West Coast fishing communities. It maintained a large, bustling store in downtown Salt Lake City, and listed on its roster members of all the professions. Stringham, mistaking the economics of necessity for the beginnings of a utopian, moneyless society, used the organization's newspaper for idealist sermonizing.

The N.D.A. issued scrip as a medium of exchange, as did many of the depression barter groups, and divided its transactions into three classes. Class A included the services of barbers, carpenters, doctors, dentists, laborers, teachers, and many others who exchanged their skills and time for scrip on a debit and credit system. Class B included goods which were exchanged on a *part cash* basis. Class C consisted of surplus goods—canned food, oil, soap, dried fruits, fish, coal, and other N.D.A. products—sold for cash to pay for those goods and services that couldn't be bartered for. The list of these is the same today, including postage, telephone, utilities, gas, taxes, and chain-store purchases.

The use of scrip in the depression had a real and positive psychological effect on its takers who tended to be liberal spenders with the funny money. One of the barbers employed in the N.D.A.'s barber and beauty section commented:

If I have money I feel like hanging on to it, but if, say, some nice cabbage comes in that I can buy for all scrip, I look at my coupons and I think, "Oh pshaw, it's only scrip anyway; I'll take some home to the neighbors."

Scrip operated in a channel through which money refused to flow, and joined together people with services and talents to surplus goods and produce without the use of cash.

In Denver, Colorado, the Unemployed Citizens' League had a membership of 34,000 people within three months of its founding in June, 1932. Food was the first concern. Farmers with crops they couldn't harvest for lack of cash to pay laborers were approached with a harvest-sharing proposition. Most accepted gladly, and a Department of Labor Statistics field worker reported: "In this way the farmers' labor problem was solved, the surplus crop went through a channel which cash sales could not have affected anyway, since the league members' purchasing power was practically nonexistent, and the farmer had a better market for the remainder of his produce."

Between July and December members of the group harvested and brought into Denver from three to four tons of food per day—potatoes, peas, cabbage, beans, onions, and carrots. After food, shelter was the major problem. The league acquired housing for about 200

WOOD—WOOD.—Good, solid, four-feet Hard Wood will be received in payment of old accounts, at this office if delivered any time previous to the *first of March* next.

Vermont Republican & Journal, Feb. 2, 1833

Hardwood, you cut it, $30 a cord, or give me half.

Massachusetts Farm Bulletin, January 9–22, 1981

members during its first year of operation by seeking out empty, dilapidated properties (this was the easy part) and approaching the owners with the offer that if they supplied the materials, the league would repair the places in return for rent-free housing for its families.

In Cheyenne, Wyoming, labor in exchange for farm produce resulted in almost 4000 jars of canned food to help barter members through the winter. In Yellow Springs, Ohio, Antioch College set up The Midwest Exchange, a barterers' stockholding corporation. In Dayton, Ohio, a group in the Tin Town slums raised rabbits and made soap. These were then bartered for needed goods.

Hundreds of wood camps sprang up all over the country where unemployed men cut cordwood for fuel. In Minneapolis 500 men worked in the outlying woods, and by early winter as many as 100 families a day were getting fuel wood deliveries. It was discovered that hundreds of people getting the firewood had no stoves. They had been sold off earlier in the

---

If there were one who lived wholly without the use of money, the State itself would hesitate to demand it of him. But the rich man—not to make any invidious comparison—is always sold to the institution which makes him rich. Absolutely speaking, the more money, the less virtue; for money comes between a man and his objects, and obtains them for him; and it was certainly no great virtue to obtain it. It puts to rest many questions which he would otherwise be taxed to answer; while the only new question which it puts is the hard but superfluous one, how to spend it. Thus his moral ground is taken from under his feet. The opportunities of living are diminished in proportion as what are called the "means" are increased.

Henry David Thoreau, *Civil Disobedience*

year for much-needed money. The minister of a Minneapolis church, Rev. George Mecklenburg, persuaded a local stove manufacturer to reopen his factory and pay his labor force with the barter group's credits. The factory ran at capacity production through the winter.

The importance of a *rural contact* was crucial to the successful depression barter groups, and without the link to the farms, attempts at exchange groups failed or were ineffective. None of the big city barter exchanges really got off the ground, and much publicity and newspaper coverage hailed barter as a faddish novelty. In the country, barter was business as usual. One depression observer remarked that "farmers have never lost the knack of dickering and swapping, but it appears that effete metropolitans had." The major problem was that city dwellers were largely in service occupations—cab drivers, printers, jewel setters, salesclerks, secretaries, mirror silverers, garment stitchers and the like—and in a tight cash situation their offered services were not essential to survival. A country dweller with a few hens or cows could always swap the eggs, butter, cream, and milk. The same is true today.

If you can wear it, eat it, take shelter in it, or burn it, you can barter it. This simple economic fact has remained valid and steady for thousands of years.

CHAPTER 2

Getting Started

You'd like to try your hand at barter, but you're not sure how to go about it. You shrink from the thought of walking up to a stranger and saying, "Want to swap something?" You can think of a thousand things you'd like to swap *for*, but not one single item you can offer in exchange.

You've probably been bartering since childhood—swapping blouses with your sister, trading a stack of too-familiar comic books to a friend in return for his

"This sweater fits like a dream, Sis."

old stack, swapping turns riding the new bike, or helping the lady next door rake her lawn in return for the grass clippings for your pet rabbit. As an adult you've bartered hundreds of times without giving it a second thought—perhaps a cord of wood for six months' worth of rides to work, a morning of watching Mrs. Twingle's toddler Herbie in exchange for her watching your Egbert last week, a trade-off with your mate of an ironed shirt for a repaired door latch. These once-in-a-while swaps arose naturally from situations of immediate necessity or opportunity, but now you want to be a conscious, full-time barterer. Here's how to get started, and some examples of other barterers' successful swaps. Remember, swaps are irresistible to many people and word travels fast, especially when there's news that no money is involved.

Starting Out

There are two fundamental rules to bartering: first, always ask "What'll you take for it?" instead of "How much?" and *always have something to trade*.

Before you rush out and start dickering, make a list of your skills, talents, training, abilities, interests, surplus goods, and made objects.

Try to list only skills you enjoy exercising; it's not much fun swapping bookkeeping chores for the things you need if you loathe ledgers and moved to the country to escape from them. If you prefer knitting fancy, intricate patterns instead of plain socks and mufflers, say so. If making an outrageously luxurious Black Forest cake appeals to you more than canning tomatoes, stick with the cake. If you can weave blankets, train dogs, teach fly-casting, cane chairs, butcher hogs, shoe horses, paint signs, repair appliances or chain saws, list these abilities—they're highly swappable.

The minor produce that has little place in the cash
market—homemade cheeses, a few baskets of berries,
a bushel or two of grapes or apples, a cord of seasoned
hardwood, a few Christmas trees, some handmade
potholders or dolls or aprons, young pigs, sheep,
calves, geese and chickens, or early zucchini, pickling
cukes or a few gallons of AA maple syrup—is great for
swapping in your community. If you own machinery
that stands idle part of the time, whether rototiller,
garden tractor, bulldozer, hay rake, sewing machine,
Cuisinart, dehydrator, ice cream freezer, or snow
blower, list it as swappable by the hour or day or
week.

If you don't have any skills you can barter, and
aren't producing any surplus crops or livestock, and
have no machinery, you still can barter your labor and
often pick up a new skill by so doing. In rural communities workers are always in demand. Tack a notice

on the door or bulletin board of the post office or general store offering a swap of your work for milk, fruit trees, stock, backhoe work—whatever you need—or leave it open-ended. A sure-fire swap in the early spring is to approach a farmer who has dairy cows or other stock and offer your help with mending fence. Helping with general farm chores is another good trading ticket. Farmers and stock-raisers often go for years without a vacation because they are tied to their animals. If you learn someone's animals and chore schedule over a period of time, you can offer to "farm-sit" for a week or two.

☞ *Try and match your skills and goods to the community needs.* It's downright difficult to trade your ability to tap dance, play the ocarina, set up an advertisement campaign, or mold plastic ashtrays in a rural community. Know the character of your area and identify its needs, then examine your store of abilities and talents and see what you've got to swap that matches up. The necessities of life—food, clothing, fuel, and shelter—are the "hard" currencies of the barter world, always in demand, and always tradable.

☞ *Recognize the necessity of a surplus.* Deliberately raise extra vegetables, fruit, rabbits, and turkeys or make something useful and beautiful specifically for bartering. The word will soon get around and the people with whom you trade will begin to count on your annual contribution, and put aside some of *their* surplus to meet your needs. Everybody has a surplus of something at times. A woman in San Andreas, California, says:

> I grow a staple crop as barter material. I have walnuts to trade for organic grains at health-food stores, for chicken and dog feed, and for our

Christmas tree. I grow garlic, too, and have traded the beautiful two-foot-long braids for such things as homemade wine, seeds, baked goods, and grapes.

☞ *Make your first swap with a friend, neighbor, or relative*. If you're shy or hesitant about that first plunge into barter, try it out on someone you know and like. The successful experience will give you courage and whet your appetite for more. The word will get around that you barter, and others' trade sensibilities will be tickled.

☞ *Exchange work*. Before the busy seasons of haying or harvesting get under way, volunteer to help your neighbor if he'll help you. Most homestead and farm jobs are easier and better done by several pairs of willing hands—canning, quilting, butchering are only a few of the annual tasks lightened by help.

☞ *Keep your eyes open for swaps*. The difference between the consistently successful barterer and the once-in-a-while swapper is that the true trader keeps his or her eyes and ears open for chances to swap. If

STOCK UP NOW
ON
ZUCCHINI
WORLD'S MOST USEFUL
VEGETABLE
COOKED, MASHED, FRIED,
BAKED INTO BREAD,
ALSO USEFUL IN BASEBALL,
SELF-DEFENSE, FLOOD CONTROL.

your neighbor sighs "I don't know why we raised so many turkeys this year. We've got fifteen of them and the freezer is already full," offer her something in trade, say an equal value of pies and cakes home-baked by your secret recipe. If you hear Old Man Grapple, the apricot grower, muttering that he wished he had a black-and-tan like his deceased Ol' Tiger, and you remember that the fellow at the end of your cousin Jake's road has a nice litter of black-and-tan pups and was heard to be looking for fence posts, and if you have an antique sleigh with one runner gone that the uncle of a fencing dealer (who happens to be distantly related to Mr. Grapple's wife) covets, and you recognize this tangle of wants and needs as a barter opportunity, you are on your way to becoming a master trader. Take the barterer's attitude that *no swap is too small*. It's the little trades that add up to a lifetime of satisfying swaps. This is the kind of everyday trading that becomes a pleasant and neighborly habit. Soon the only time you'll pull out your money is when you go to town.

But there are dozens of other ways to get into swapping than direct one-to-one trades—your pumpkins for my peanuts. Some of these other barter forms may suit you or your community better than direct exchange.

Community Barter Groups

If your area has a barter organization already going, you are ahead of the game before you start, for here is a group of congenial folk eager to trade with you. Community barter organizations come in all sizes and forms; some are started and sponsored by church or civic groups, some are the brainstorms of devoted individuals who provide the organizational fire, some are "alternate living" ventures connected with a commune or co-op, some are geared to suit certain members of the community such as senior citizens or Saturday afternoon school children, or collectors of antique cannons.

Useful Services Exchange of Reston, Virginia, is a community barter oganization founded several years ago by retired economist Henry Ware. This group, whose membership is drawn from middle-class Reston inhabitants in that Washington suburb, has a central office that makes the initial contact between members. No goods are swapped. Instead members barter the hard-to-find skills and services. These are the small repair jobs that no contractor will touch, a ride into the city for a shopping trip, visit to the hairdresser, or to a meeting (especially helpful and needed by elderly people who no longer drive or keep a car), the loan of a punch bowl or coffee maker around the community entertainment circuit, baby-sitting, house-sitting, and a hundred other convenient services all collected in a central file for the use of the community's enthusiastic barterers.

Give and Take of Burlington, Vermont, is another kind of barter group, founded by the Burlington Ecumenical Action Ministry, an interdenominational church organization. Give and Take was started to bring the unemployed, welfare recipients, and people with low incomes into a community marketplace where they could exchange their skills and labor for services and goods without cash. The group's membership varies from 75 to 400, depending on the current needs of the trading community, and takes as its motto St. Paul's statement, ". . . every man shall receive his own reward according to his own labor." The members' skills and services are listed in a quarterly catalog for a fee of $3. (There are the usual overhead expenses that must be paid in cash.) The range is broad.

The offers, or GIVES, in a recent listing include: a Frisbee partner, soup cooking instructions, house painting, yard work, a subscription to any environmental publication, bread baking, VW repairs and maintenance, carpentry, canning, knitting instructions, a chain saw and operator, errands for the elderly, storage space, a fenced meadow, flat stones, sand, Sheetrock taping, goat kids, quilts and potholders, light hauling, a window-caulking service, wood splitting, and cow milking.

The other side of the swaps are TAKES, the services and things members need. These include homemade bread, handmade mittens, honey, maple syrup, transportation, kitchen supplies, rust spots on a car fixed, shelves put up, the outside of a mobile home washed and waxed, the use of a tent, a Skilsaw, a camera, a weekend at a camp, mulch hay, a ceiling painted, and windows washed.

Give and Take holds monthly swap parties with entertainment. The performers pick up their pay from a swap table loaded with produce, baked goods, and other tradable items.

A Colorado church group, Grow, has a swap table near the front door of the church where members place surplus garden produce for swapping. (If people without a garden or tradable produce take something from the barter table, they are asked to donate spare change to the church's national hunger fund.)

Many community organizations hold swap parties as ice-breakers among members, or as an adjunct to a fund-raising affair. If you are interested in starting a barter group, Give and Take offers information and advice in a special barter packet. See *Sources* at the end of this book.

FRIENDLY SWAPPING

The small swaps back and forth between neighbors and friends make life pleasant, resources convenient, and work efficient. Here's an example of the easy back-and-forth flow of barter in a small North Carolina town.

"An elderly neighbor . . . gives me the use of his tractor and tiller in exchange for their maintenance and repair. I recently rebuilt his tiller motor, and I'm really looking forward to using the machine in my garden this season.

"For the past few years I've been doing electrical maintenance for another friend. In turn, he has given me access to every carpentry tool he owns. You name it, and he's got it: routers, band saw, vises, sanders, and dowling jig. . . . It's a woodworker's paradise.

". . . I have a friend down the road who has a sawmill . . . and he occasionally needs my skills. Just the other day I installed a tape player in his car, and he came up with a supply of cedar boards for me."

Swap Boxes

Swap boxes are everywhere in California, whose residents are highly inclined to swapping. They are outside restaurants, health-food stores, general stores, and community centers. A swap box is a large, sturdy wooden box with a cover. People put in clothing and small objects they no longer have use for, and pick out in return marvelous hats, blouses, fripperies, cowboy boots, string hammocks, blue jeans, sweaters, and sunglasses in a kind of informal series of running swaps. Some diligent devotees of the swap boxes manage to refurbish their annual wardrobes without going near a store or spending money.

In Cambridge, Massachusetts, California's swap boxes become Free Boxes—big wooden bins outside community and church buildings where clothing is traded. One patron of the Cambridge Free Boxes comments:

> Now I take that dress I never wear, or that shirt somebody gave me that's two sizes too big, and just drop it off in one of the Free Boxes. When I get in the mood for some new clothes, I don't waste money . . . I just rummage around in the Free Box and pick up what I need.

A different kind of swap box is located at a hiker's hostel in Hot Springs, North Carolina, along the Appalachian Trail. Scott Feierabend and his wife of Baton Rouge, Louisiana, described it in a letter to *Mother Earth News:*

> Whatever a person didn't want or could no longer use was placed in a large carton. These contributions included not only every sort of on-the-trail food imaginable, but soap, rope, books, candles,

and a variety of backpacking equipment. After "shopping" through the box, an individual would replace what he took with whatever unwanted goodies *he* might have.

We were so impressed with the system that *we* established a swap box at a trail stop farther north.

A California woman started a community swap box when her favorite thrift shop closed its doors. Here's how she did it:

First, I acquired a large plywood crate and painted the words "Free Box" on all sides. Then I contributed some of my unneeded clothing to the container and—with the permission of the owner—placed the carton behind our local natural-food store.

Next, I spread the word of potential swaps and—before I knew it—the box was full . . . overflowing with an interesting assortment of near-perfect clothes, toys, and appliances, all free for the taking.

. . . Moreover, the center requires a minimum of maintenance. A weekly check to cull the "unwanted unwanteds" for contribution to the thrift shop of a neighboring town is all it takes.

If you want to start a swap box, pick the nearest general store or garage—some place many people visit during the week—and ask the owner's permission to park a swap box out front. Make sure it's out of the weather or has a waterproof cover. You can get it off to a good start by taking up a "starter" collection among friends and neighbors to stock it. Every few weeks be sure to check the contents and weed out any "doggy" items that are taking up space. If somebody has donated something impossibly stained, faded, and ripped, put it aside until you have a collection of rags and donate a bagful to the local garage, where rags are always needed.

The Barter Party

A barter party can run from a simple get-together of a small bunch of like-minded friends for an evening of trading and pot-luck supper, to a publicized commu-

---

William Colston, Painter of houses, carriages, signs, glazing, paper hanging, makes chairs, French and common bedsteads, and many other articles of Cabinet work. Will sell very low for Cash, Lumber, or Produce. White and grey Lime wanted.

Vermont Republican & Journal, Jan. 21, 1832

nity activity or an all-day barter bazaar at a cooperating farm.

In one small Minnesota town a circle of friends meets with every change of the seasons to swap unused but attractive garments with each other as a "clothes exchange party." The women take turns sifting through the clothes rack, and trying on the clothes. After a few hours of "shopping," conversation, and renewed friendships, each ends up happily with new clothes for free. Other groups hold annual or seasonal swaps of children's clothes—sturdy but outgrown garments that cost an arm and a leg new. These cooperative, social gatherings recycle garments that might otherwise be discarded, and save hundreds of dollars as well as the hassle of expensive and frustrating shopping excursions.

In North Dakota an elementary school teacher who wanted to put across the idea of recycling and saving our resources in a graphic way, held a barter day. Each child took to school an object from home that had been headed for the trash can. The items were on

"That's certainly a realistic doll, Alice."

display for the morning, then in the afternoon some heavy swapping began.

What a success! My students brought in all sorts of things to trade: books, magazines, records, radios, craft objects, stuffed animals, toys, games, etc. The children quickly learned the value and fun of trading rather than dumping.

The Richards family at their Moon-Star Farm in Newburg, Oregon, raises walnuts, apples, and cherries. A year ago at harvest time they decided to try a Barter Bazaar on the farm, and sent out flyers to notify swappers. It was a good experience, for people came from all around the region, bringing pottery, geese, ducks, herbs, clothing, and hundreds of other items to swap. The Richards thought the whole thing was great, and intend to do it again.

Barter parties of recyclable goods are excellent activities for groups—ladies' auxiliary organizations, youth groups such as scouts and 4-H'ers, senior citizens' centers, hospital wards, volunteer fire departments. When people gather, no other excuse is needed to start swapping.

The Barter Fair

A barter fair is a barter party enlarged to huge dimensions. One of the most famous is the three-day annual Northeast Washington Barter and Harvest Festival, which in five years has grown from a few hundred produce, craft, and skill swappers to several thousand hard-bartering traders. The fair is held in a different place each year to equalize the distance swappers must drive to attend the doings. Pickup trucks, old vans, and even wagons, all bulging with

squash, pumpkins, grapes, baskets, homespun wool, and many other products of the land and hands of Washington, make their way to this barterers' holiday every autumn. One family which has been to every one of the fairs brings its old cider press and a ton or more of zesty apples gathered free from the wilds. They press more than 100 gallons of fresh sweet cider and swap for onions, keeper potatoes, garlic, melons, squash, dried fruit, and a hundred other items, including in the past, *two* kitchen sinks.

A news sheet from the festival tells the producer of minor produce that the barter fair will "provide a way for us to sell or trade the products we've grown or made . . . without having to resort to the conventional market system, in which producers are too often cheated." More to the point is that here suddenly is an excellent market for local produce and goods where none existed before.

Not only organic gardeners and orchardists go to the barter fair. Craftsmen, from a blacksmith with a traveling forge who makes tools to order on the spot, to weavers of delicate grass baskets, makers of leather goods, spinners of wool, sewers and knitters of garments in a gorgeous rainbow of colors from sharp magenta to the misty lichen-greys and rose madders of natural plant dyes, are all there swapping for some of the finest produce grown in the country.

There are dozens of apple varieties from the famous Washington orchards; deep crimson tomatoes, pear-shaped ones, Big Boys, Pixies, cherry tomatoes; jars of green tomato chutney; huge and tender broccoli nestled in blue-green leafage the color of distant mountains; baskets brimming with ripe plums, pears, melons, and grapes; glowing heaps of ruddy pumpkins— all the variety and color of produce the most demanding gourmet ever dreamed of. Fresh popcorn a-poppin', generous helpings of creamy yogurt ladled out of big tubs a dairy commune took to the fair along with homemade cheeses in an astounding range of colors and shapes and flavors, breads of every nationality from squat round loaves of Russian Black to long cigars of crusty French bread. Hand mills grind out fresh cornmeal and flour on the spot, pumpkin and

---

WHAT TO TRADE

Best Trading Goods	Worst Trading Goods
Land	Plastic products
Gold and Silver	Gas-guzzling cars
Cordwood	Mattresses
Plumbing, carpentry labor	Zucchini (in season)
Tools	Books of poetry
Pickup trucks	Broken appliances
Sporting goods	Used refrigerators

"... and thou?"

sunflower seeds are toasted before your eyes, crunchy granola and cracked wheat and dozens of other grain products are bartered up and down this open air marketplace. If you've got something to trade, this is the place to take it.

At the end of the busy trading day, participants in the barter fair donate food items. They are carried by a mule to the central kitchen where volunteers cook vast amounts of food to feed 2,000 hungry swappers. A bluegrass band and dancing near a central campfire add to the day's pleasures.

If you want to start a barter fair, here are a few tips. A harvest barter festival, like the Northeast Washington Harvest and Barter Festival, is almost a natural event where growers can swap surplus produce in exchange for things they didn't grow. But a spring barter fair can also be successful with seeds, flats of started seedlings, nursery stock, onion sets, houseplants, seed potato, bagged compost, dried manure, gardening books, cuttings, advice from experienced growers, pots from local potters, scions from superior fruit trees, gardening tools and carts, seed catalog swaps, and whatever inventive gardening swappers offer. A barter festival can be geared to crafts alone, or to musical instruments, or to livestock and poultry. Decide what kind of barter fair would go well in your region, and think what kind of a draw you want. It could attract just local people, the whole county, or even the entire state or a multi-state region.

When you've decided on the type, place, and time for your barter fair, *don't* just tack up posters at random and plunk an ad into the paper. You want serious barterers and producers, not summer people and gawkers who will come empty-handed and try to buy for money instead of swapping their own goods. Advertise at co-ops, put posters up at rural and farm-supply stores, spread the word among the kind of people you want to attract. Much of the success of the Northeast Washington Barter and Harvest Festival is linked to the kind of people the festival draws— hardworking country people dedicated to the land and its uses who bring what they've grown or made themselves. Barter is a way of life with many of these traders.

Start small. Don't try to attract a huge crowd the first year. The idea will catch on and your barter fair will grow if it's a repeat event. A local harvest barter fair is probably the easiest way to begin. It's a lot of hard work for the organizers, but what rewards!

WHAT YOU NEED FOR A BARTER FAIR

• *A site:* an empty field, a dry meadow, a parking lot, a village common, and athletic field, an empty fairground, and permission to use it.

• *Permission from town authorities.* Anything that draws a crowd usually needs some kind of traffic control. If the proposed site for your barter fair is near or in a village, find out the local rules. Talk to the selectmen and constable before you start putting up posters.

• *Volunteers.* Somebody has to lay out and mark the parking areas. (Keep the barter area itself restricted to booths and tables with no vehicles unless heavy loads mean admittance to the inner circle.)

Somebody has to make all those little signs that point to the toilet, the barter area, the lost and found. A camping area for overnight swappers who come long distances may be necessary. They'll need water, toilets, and permission to build fires. An outhouse or portable toilet on The Day is a necessity, as well as a drinking water supply and a wash-up area and first-aid station. Someone has to put up the posters and go around telling the right people about the upcoming fair. (Try to choose outgoing people, good talkers with persuasive, twinkly eyes.)

If you allow fires and cooking, you'll have to lay in a supply of dry wood—for barter, of course. You'll need a few shifts of volunteers to walk around during the fair and make sure nobody is trading genuine snake oil for gold bars. Unlike rock concerts and other Good-Time-Charlie outdoor events, a barter fair attracts serious, interested, participating swappers instead of bored rowdies looking for amusement.

• *A central bulletin board* for announcements and special events can tell folks where, when, how and what, and pull the gathering together.

Bartering for Medical and Dental Care and Legal Advice

Most professionals are eager swappers and good traders. There are so many accounts of dentists and doctors bartering their services for office repainting jobs that it's possible no medico in the entire country has paid cash for a paint job.

One of the most successful was a young couple's swap with an upstate Vermont pediatrician in a small town—a year's medical care of their numerous children in return for a zany and imaginative paint job of stripes, pointing fingers, ridiculous signs, painted ants following the leader, and dozens of eye-catching visual puzzles in lively colors. Both sides were delighted with their good deal.

Another couple in Wichita, Kansas, who enjoy looking for Indian arrowheads and artifacts, have become quite skillful in unearthing these objects from a vanished past. They found that their dentist also had a keen interest in local archaeology, but was tied to his office during daylight hours, rarely getting the chance to dig. Bartering and a friendship were a natural result. They started off by swapping an Indian war club for a gold crown, and kept on trading.

An experienced trader in Texas needed $500 worth of work on his teeth, but the first dentist he tried wasn't a barterer. Undaunted, he tried another, an excellent man at a nearby dental clinic and laboratory who swapped him a full upper plate and a four-tooth bottom partial for a yearling heifer.

Another dentist, when asked if he'd barter for needed work, told Charles Wolf, Jr., of Milford, Ohio, who was up for some crown work, that he needed firewood and would swap for all he could get. Mr. Wolf had neither woodlot nor fireplace himself, but bustled about and made a few inquiries in the style of the determined barterer, discovering no less than ten

"Better make that two cords of wood. Sounds like twins."

places where he could sharecrop firewood, as well as all the cut-down trees along a state highway free for carrying them away.

Obstetricians and midwives are probably the medical people who do the most swapping. Often their patients are young, with little cash but plenty of energy and willingness. One couple in Missouri ran up a $450 obstetrical bill for the birth of their first child, and had hardly made a dent in it before they realized they were facing an additional bill of the same nature.

The father had noticed the doctor's car was a hiccupping clunker, so he hesitantly offered his mechanic services in overhauling the vehicle in return for the money owed and about to be owing. Although the obstetrician was reluctant at first, she thought better of it the next time she drove her car. Soon the young father was making road calls to rescue the doctor in her roadside disasters. He overhauled the transmission and put the heap into sturdy running condition in return for the obstetrical care.

In Redwood City, California, a couple swapped a homemade down comforter, two down covers, and a stained glass window to a doctor for attending at the births of their two children.

Veterinarians have a streak of barter, also. In New York State a couple's beloved German shepherd dog was hit by a school bus and had to have part of one hind leg amputated at a very healthy cost. The couple explained that they were indeed rich, but in organic farm produce and livestock rather than money, and asked the vet if he'd like to swap. The bargain was struck, and the vet got home-grown, butchered, and cured bacon, pork chops, and roasts, some honey, braided strings of onions and garlic, some pumpkins, gourds, and dried flowers while the dog recovered from his accident and the surgery. A good swap for everyone.

Country lawyers are good barterers. Don't hesitate to ask. One Seattle, Washington, lawyer, who frequently swaps his services for goods, once traded drawing up an elderly lady's will for a pint jar of homemade rhubarb wine and a little conversation every Friday afternoon for the rest of her days. The lawyer wrote: "It was a sad Friday indeed when the wine stopped coming . . . and the Will had to serve its purpose."

A city-bound lawyer, Patrick M.G. Prosser of Lexington, Kentucky, describes himself as "a barterin' fool" and trades his professional advice with a farmer in the countryside who boards and pastures the lawyer's five horses. He swaps legal work with the blacksmith for shoeing the same beasts, ditto with the vet who treats them, and the same with the tack shop for

"It's a little hard to think of you as not guilty of auto theft when you offer to pay me with a new Mercedes."

supplies, saddlery, and horsey equipment. He remarks:

Folks who need the services of such people as doctors, lawyers, vets, and accountants shouldn't hesitate to offer a swap for labor or skills or products. It never hurts to make such a suggestion. . . and in most cases you'll find that professionals appreciate the beauty of barter—and enjoy the definite feeling of goodwill that always exists between folks who trade—just as much as anyone else.

Amen.

TRADING TIPS

A Vermont midwife works for about 50 percent cash and 50 percent barter. After a few not entirely satisfactory experiences she has worked out a few guidelines and traded her work for honey and meat, a down comforter, three matched bookcases, electrical and carpentry work, and custom-designed place mats, each not only a good swap, but a treasured memento of the happy occasion when she's helped bring a new baby into the world. Her rules are:

☞ Never take in trade anything you don't like, don't want, or have absolutely no use for. You'll only end up feeling ripped off . . . and this will cause resentment in your later dealings.

☞ Be explicit in your agreements. Specify what you're going to do and what you expect in return.

☞ Set a time limit for the completion of the exchange.

All good advice, though many canny barterers take items they neither need nor like in swaps if they think they can trade them with a third party—the famous barter triangulation.

Barter Co-ops

Barter co-ops are small local groups usually restricted to one *type* of barter service. The most common are baby-sitting co-ops, local transportation co-ops, home repair and maintenance swappers (my plumbing services for your electrical repairs), and such arrangements as keeping someone else's lawn mowed and hedge trimmed during a vacation, a service reciprocated when you take your annual holiday.

Baby-sitting co-ops are popular and offer a real break to harried women who crave a few hours to

themselves—to keep doctor and dentist appointments, run errands without sticky, clutching fingers, take a music lesson or an academic course free from dragging little Squillkins along. Such an arrangement has rewards other than privacy and free time for mother. The children enjoy contact with new or favorite playmates and like swapping toys, and pre-schoolers are exposed to a small group environment without the expense or institutional environment of a formal nursery school.

Holly Freeman of Yamhill, Oregon, belongs to a baby-sitting co-op which has worked out a good system. She suggests that notices about setting up a baby-sitting co-op be posted on the feed store, grocery market and church bulletin boards to draw interested women together. A few meetings may be necessary to set out some basic rules on what's expected in caring for another's children.

This group issues scrip—two-inch squares of colored construction paper. Each member of the co-op starts out with twenty units of scrip, each representing half an hour of baby-sitting for one child. A few coffee gatherings at the beginning introduce all the mothers and children to each other. Arrangements are made privately without a central coordinator, but if someone runs out of scrip, she lets other members know that she'd appreciate first consideration when a sitter is needed. The scrip circulates until it's nearly worn out, then "new money" is issued at a general meeting and the Yamhill Baby-Sitting Co-op continues its satisfying round of specialized barter. Another Oregon baby-sitting co-op keeps books of credits and debits for hours of child care instead of issuing scrip.

Either simple and workable system can be applied to any situation that calls for ongoing, often-needed local services, from trips to town to brush-cutting.

Sharecropping

Sharecropping is one of mankind's most ancient forms of barter. All historical eras have had sharecroppers and shared crops. The whaling and sealing entrepreneurs of the last century paid their hands in shares of the venture's profits, down to complex fractions of a "lay," as the shares were called. A large percentage of the whaling profits—for example, the captain's share—was called "a short lay" while a meager share was "a long lay." Although the historical abuses of sharecropping have given the practice a certain notoriety, for many people it is a highly workable and gratifying form of barter. In a classic sharecropping situation, a farmer brings only his and his family's labor to the bargain; the landlord supplies the land, housing for the sharecropper, seed, tools, and equipment, and often credit for needed living expenses. At harvest time the sharecropper is paid off in shares of the harvest crop, usually 50 percent, with the landlord taking the other half.

Modern sharecroppers may prefer to keep such barters small and simple—tending or caring for someone else's orchard, hayfield, vegetable garden, beehives, citrus groves, or rhubarb patch "on the halves" or "on the quarters."

An Arkansas beekeeper has hives placed in strategic spots all over his rural community, and regularly swaps honey with the farmers where his bees pasture, for the right to set out his hives.

One farmer who specialized in soybeans also had a number of heavily producing pecan trees, but didn't have time to care for them. He already had a good supply of honey and didn't need more, so the beekeeper worked out a sharecropping arrangement. He and his family would gather the pecan harvest "on the halves." In only a few afternoons they got a year's supply of delicious pecans as well as Christmas gifts for less ingenious relatives and friends, and supplied the farmer with bushels of plump nuts for *his* use.

In Puerto Rico a young and newly married couple with very little money noticed, on a walk through their area, a gorgeous cherry tree whose upper branches were thick with clustered crimson fruits. After much hesitating, they knocked on the door of the house and suggested to the elderly lady who answered that they pick the cherries on shares. The woman agreed, remarking that she could only pick the lower branches because she was afraid she might fall if she went higher up into the tree. The couple went home and collected boxes, bags, dishpans, and pails, then picked delicious ripe cherries to overflowing. They took home a bag of warm cookies the tree owner baked while they picked.

Through want of enterprise and faith men are where they are, buying and selling, and spending their lives like serfs.

Henry David Thoreau

In later years they discovered many fruit-laden trees owned by older people reluctant to risk climbing into the upper branches to harvest their fruit, and have made a good thing of picking on shares.

Thousands of landless gardeners and no-time landowners have gotten together in recent years in sharecropping situations. If you have land standing idle, put the word around that you're willing to barter on sharecrop terms. If you have ripe grain, corn, or fruit or mature garden produce that you can't gather yourself, share the harvest with someone who'll pick it for you. If you dislike the stoop-labor of digging autumn potatoes, or if you're busy with more urgent tasks or have an injury, sharecrop the digging out. Put up a notice at the local gathering place:

Laid up and can't dig my potatoes. Will go shares with good digger. Stop by Google's farm on the River Road. 'Tater fork supplied.

Advice, Information, and Help

Getting and giving advice is a big part of country barter. This swapping pays off not only in knowledge and skill, but in good feelings and happy human relations and makes your community a better place to live (if possible).

Mr. and Mrs. LeeRoy Sheffield of Stonington, Illinois, are semi-disabled, but they have a big garden, keep rabbits, chickens, ducks, and geese. They are also excellent cooks. On Sundays their custom is to prepare a monstrous dinner for twenty to twenty-five people and invite young relatives and their friends to swap some work for the dinner. For a few hours of weeding in the garden, repairing and washing the cars, roof-mending, killing and plucking the chickens and

"What's Spanish for baby-sitting?"

rabbits for the feast, and other needed jobs, the
helpers enjoy all they can eat, then polish off the day
with badminton, croquet, or volleyball.

A couple on an Ontario farm in a Mennonite farming
community pitched in along with all the neighbors to
plant, grow, and harvest the crops of a farmer who had
an accident at planting time and was laid up in the
hospital for months. In the same community after a
barn burned, everyone turned out the next day to raise
a new one. Such cooperative rural community efforts
are better than insurance.

In California a couple learned that their new Mexi-
can-origin neighbors were having difficulties filling out
the dozens of forms—for schools, taxes, Social Security—that our bureaucratic society demands. Their
English simply was not up to the task. In exchange for
help with the paperwork, the couple got "anytime"
baby-sitting service and some long and fascinating
conversations about Mexican culture.

The elderly are often overlooked in our society, parked in the old age home or nursing home or in front of a television set as though all the years they have lived and all the experiences of a long life counted for nothing. In rural communities the old people are more apt to remain a vital part of the area's life, and are a valuable source of useful information, especially to new farmers and homesteaders coming into the country for the first time. They know from first-hand experience all the tricks of farming, logging, gardening, fruit-growing, what varieties do well in the climate, where the area's frost pockets lie, where the old roads ran, wildlife habitats, berry patches, good trout holes, and lost boundary lines. Many of them have forgotten more about horseflesh and cows than the county agent ever knew. They can give instruction in skilled needlework, and are sources of unusual recipes, local folklore, and history. The *Foxfire* books were originally a school project to gather in the disappearing information and skills stored in the heads and hands of the elderly members of an Appalachian community, a body of knowledge sorely needed by the emerging wave of new small farmers. Hundreds of people have "discovered" the rich banks of information in the minds and memories of the rural elderly.

In North Carolina an elderly farmer can no longer trust his reaction time well enough to drive. In swap for chauffeuring services the two miles to town he lets his young neighbors harvest tomatoes, potatoes, beets, peas, lettuce, and other produce from his vast garden. In Michigan an old lady who cannot drive gives her young neighbor weekly lessons in fancy knitting, crocheting, sewing, and soapmaking in return for a trip to market once a week. In California another elderly woman, who can no longer manage the heavy work of canning, donated her meat grinder, canning jars, pressure canner, cold packer, and food mill to a

young woman who had garden produce, time, and
strength, but no canning equipment, in return for a
share of the canned goods, some basic housecleaning
chores, and weekly baking. A retired farmer in New
Hampshire swaps the use of his acres for hay crops
and animal pasturage with his younger neighbors. A
skilled quilt-piecer, whose eyesight is no longer good
enough for fine stitchery, swaps instruction in quilting
and special patterns of traditional coverlets. A retired
Vermont butter maker who ran a home dairy for sixty
years passes on the skills and tricks of a lifetime to a
neighbor with his first cow in return for some of the
butter and seasoned cordwood. A New Hampshire
lumberjack in his eighties explains to a young log cabin
builder how he cut dovetail notches with an ax in trade
for a rare restaurant dinner.

Old country people, the greatest untapped source on
rural living, people who have lived through drought,
flood, two world wars, the depression, who weathered
the long decades of farm workers and families leaving
the land for the cities, now see the tide turning back,

and the children and grandchildren of those who left and lost their country knowledge, returning to the land.

Barter Directories and Specialized Exchanges

Most barter organizations and clubs publish a quarterly directory for a fee, listing members' needs and wants as well as the goods and talents they offer. Yet there need not be a formal organization behind a barter directory; a community or church listing, or a mimeographed booklet setting out local gives and takes can be put together by one person, for a fee or for free. A few volunteers can get a community barter directory rolling.

The simplest form of barter directory is a community bulletin board of good size where proposed swaps can be chalked or pinned up but changed easily and frequently. Swap lists are usually headed "Needs" and "Have." Many magazines and country publications, from newspapers and newsletters to shoppers, run swappers' columns. One of the best-known and oldest is "The Original Yankee Swopper's Column," which has run since the Forties in *Yankee* magazine. Fifty randomly drawn swaps are run each month along with seventy-five genealogical information swaps. Here are a few recent samples:

I have an original travel brochure, preserved and framed, for the maiden voyage of the Titanic, written 1911. Want antique, large, good condition rolltop desk and chair.

Have old brass and glass German Draft lottery tumbler filled with wooden name pellets to swop for Ithaca calendar clock.

Swop large collection Horatio Alger books for Johnson 5 HP outboard motor in good condition with gas tank.

Seek info/desc. George Bachmann, Hessian soldier in Rev. War, discharged 1781, N.Y.C. area.

Small Farmer's Journal, published in Oregon, has a column listing FARMER'S SEEDS with the offer:

Any farmers who have seed of their own raising to sell or trade may advertise here free of charge. No company or business ads. We want to encourage the preservation of plant diversity. . . .

Antique dealers and collectors of everything from muzzle-loading pistols to old barbed wire are almost always seasoned barterers well used to trading, since many of the rarer pieces can only be traded for and never bought. Special publications catering to the interests of these groups often carry exchange ads, but if you know something about the value and rarity of the item you're swapping, never hesitate to barter with these advertisers. They enjoy a good dicker more than most, and although they may be an "advanced" group for a beginning swapper, it's a good way to learn, as a satisfied Maine woman found out back in the depression when she swapped a fancy gilt-finished toilet seat for an antique pump organ with a dealer in antiques. She's been enjoying the instrument ever since. We hope he's as satisfied.

House Swaps

A common barter arrangement is to swap your maintenance and repair skills on the upkeep of a dilapidated old house with the owner for rent-free tenancy. While many of these deals work out, some don't, and it's best to have a clear understanding *in writing* of who is responsible for what. One couple in northern New England casually agreed to "fix up" an old, uninsulated house in return for free rent. In a cold snap when temperatures plunged to forty below, the pipes froze and burst. The owner insisted the couple replace the pipes and insulate them. After much palaver the problem was resolved by sharing costs for the project. But when strong winds ripped off a section of the decayed shingle roof, the owner insisted the couple reroof the entire house at their own expense. It was a job that would cost them hundreds of dollars in material and several weeks of labor on the steepest roof pitch in the county. They found another place to live.

But for hundreds of other people maintenance-for-a-roof works well. A Massachusetts woman owns a camp in New Hampshire which she can only use on occasional weekends and vacations. She thought about bartering tenancy in the cabin for some upkeep work on it, but hated to lose even the sporadic use of the place. When she mentioned her problem to a friend she discovered *he* was looking for an inexpensive place to rent in New Hampshire near his college, and planned to go home to his parents' house on most weekends. It was a good swap, and within a month the cabin sported a new porch and deck complete with shingled roof built by the caretaker-tenant.

Somewhat different was the case of the couple who were stony broke after buying their coveted piece of land, and had no house to live in. A nearby neighbor had an old log barn that he wanted to replace with a snappy new metal number, and offered the old barn to the young couple if they'd take it down and haul the logs away. By the end of the summer the log barn had been transported and rebuilt into a snug little house on their property for little more than the effort of getting it there and putting it back together.

A Colorado couple bought twenty-five acres of un-improved land in the country a few years ago and watched the land appreciate in value as time went by. Unfortunately, building costs rose even faster than land values, and they couldn't see a way to build their house. But when they were introduced to a local con-tractor who was longing for a few acres in the country for his own place, the swap almost made itself. They traded five acres of their land to the contractor, who built them a custom-designed house on their favorite knoll. Both parties were delighted with this major bar-ter transaction that house two families without a penny changing hands.

One ingenious repairs-for-rent barter deal was care-fully planned. A couple built up their homestead nest egg by remodeling houses. When they were ready to look for land to buy in eastern Oregon, they had a problem—no place to stay, and not enough money for a standard rental agreement. At their local library they found the names of a dozen eastern Oregon news-papers, then sent each a classified ad reading: "Handy-man will trade free rent for renovating your old home." Out of five good responses they found the perfect swap—a house in a small town in the middle of Oregon whose Seattle owners gave them a free hand with re-pairs.

> The trade turned out really well for everyone in-volved. Our barter partners got several thousand dollars' worth of repair work done—for free—on their empty house. And we got six months of no-rent living, a chance to sharpen our recently ac-quired remodeling skills, and plenty of spare time to drive around and find our future home. . . .

WANTED: VACATION SWAP.
ESCAPE SUMMER'S HEAT.

Some clever house-hunters drive around an area they like looking for old, untenanted houses, find out who the owners are, and suggest a fix-it-up-for-free-rent barter deal. Often it works out to everyone's satisfaction.

There is a different kind of house-swapping—mutual trade organizations for vacationers and travelers. One couple, who subscribes to a vacation exchange club, recently arranged successive swaps with house-traders in Detroit, Spain, Indonesia, Australia, New Zealand, and California.

Most vacation house exchange clubs publish, for a fee, a directory listing people all over the world who want to swap their apartments, country houses, camps, and cabins to others for a return swap. Many times the barter includes use of vehicles and boats. In 1978 more than 3,000 Americans swapped houses for periods ranging from a few weeks to several months with fellow traders all over the world. There are advantages in arranging a house swap through an organization—a large number of choices, ease and efficiency, plus club information on sample written agreement forms, on insurance coverage and a dozen minor arrangements that make the exchange pleasant for both parties.

Here is advice on house-swapping if you think you'd like to exchange your country corner for one in Ireland or Spain for a few weeks. A listing of the major house-swapping organizations can be found at the end of this book.

IF YOU WANT TO SWAP YOUR HOUSE

☛ Start looking for a prospective house swap a good three or four months before your vacation. You may have to write and telephone a number of contacts before you find the right house exchange.

☛ Before the swap actually takes place settle these details:

Decide what to do about accidental damage, telephone charges, electricity bills, food and liquor supplies.

Tell whom to contact in case repairs are needed on appliances, plumbing, or the house itself.

Pack away fragile objects and heirlooms before the guests arrive.

Leave instructions for operating everything from the sump pump to the thermostat.

Post an emergency phone number where you can be reached.

☛ Thoughtful swappers leave a prepared meal for the hungry strangers who may arrive late at night or when restaurants are all closed.

House-swapping relationships can become as mellow and long-lasting as those between neighborly barter partners if you pick out someone who enjoys your place as much as you enjoy his.

—◆—◆◆◆—◆—

H.M. Bates & Co. of Hartland, Vt.:
Dress goods & Drugs & Medicines—WANTED—*Cheese, Butter, Flannel Cloths*, Flaxseed *Snake* and *Blood-root, Ergot*, &c.

Vermont Republican & Journal, Jan. 14, 1832

—◆—◆◆◆—◆—

WHO SHOULD BARTER?

☞ If you have a restricted income or are on Social Security, if you are a scholarship student, are unemployed, work part-time, or are a welfare recipient, barter can *change your life*. By swapping your skills, services, and goods, you can earn many of life's necessities and luxuries without cash money.

☞ If you are a small farm owner or operator, a homesteader, an artist or craftsperson, if you are barred from the job market because of age, because you are disabled, or have no transportation, barter is for you and can put you into brisk trading circulation.

"Here's the deal. You give me an 'A' and I won't drive you crazy.
After all, what's your mind worth?"

☞ If your area is economically depressed and unemployment is high, if inflation is gobbling your cash faster than you can make it, barter is a way out of these dead ends. *Barter is inflation-proof*.

☞ If your business can't get off the ground for lack of customers, barter organizations, clubs, and exchanges can put you in touch with hundreds of potential contacts.

☞ If you can't find anyone to repair your leaky roof, to mend your torn and buttonless clothes, to fix watches and small appliances, to paint your shutters and weed your tulip bed, a services exchange or a skillsbank is the answer.

☞ If you're sick and tired of the consumer rat race, if you feel you're in a money-earning, bill-paying rut, creative barter is your escape hatch.

☞ If you hate keeping up with the Joneses and the money mentality that slaps a price tag on everything, you're ready for barter.

☞ If you are lonely, if the world seems full of greedy, selfish people interested only in themselves and the possessions they acquire, barter will involve you in rewarding personal relationships.

CHECKLIST FOR FIRST-TIME SWAPPERS

☞ *Know what you've got to barter*. Clean out the trunks in the attic, look in the back room. Do you have a spare room, an empty cellar, a rider-mower that sits idle six days a week? Can you baby-sit, type, drive, read aloud? Do you do needlework, have firewood, garden produce, goat milk, baby pigs? Make a list—these are your barter assets.

☞ *Start with a neighbor, relative, or friend*. Start small, also. A successful, easy, first barter experience will give you plenty of enthusiasm for more.

☞ *Don't say yes without a little bargaining*. Novice traders tend to get rattled easily and agree to lopsided trades because they are flustered. Stay cool and judicious and make a counteroffer. On the other hand, if you open negotiations with a neighbor and he or she looks surprised and stammers,

"No, I can't barter," don't give up. Try again another day—it takes a little while for most people to get used to new ideas. "Try it, you'll like it," is a good barter ice-breaking phrase.

☞ *Be sure everything is crystal clear.* Who delivers what when? A long delay in a swap delivery is very discouraging to the one who's waiting. Any materials or travel that must be paid in cash should be agreed on. Once you give your word, keep it scrupulously.

☞ *Try to think beyond the one-to-one swap.* So what if you don't like the frilly organdy aprons Mrs. Fudge wants to trade you; hold onto them a while and you'll find a swapper who does want them.

☞ *Don't turn down money if it's offered.* A lot of new barterers reject offers of cash as though it were tainted with plague germs. Money has its uses. You can always buy something and trade *that*.

☞*Keep your eyes open* for swap opportunities wherever you go; they're there, all around you.

CHAPTER 3

Creative Bartering

Generations of tales and regional jokes about Yankee traders and sharp Connecticut swappers who palmed off wooden hams and nutmegs on more credulous folk, or bartered hollow watch cases with click beetles inside to trusting bumpkins, have established even in modern minds the image of the barterer as a shifty-eyed, fast-talking, swift-footed dissembler who could paint a black horse white and swap it back to the same farmer he'd stolen it from. Most of these unsavory characters are long gone, but a few linger in profitable back corners. Wherever there's the smell of gain there are a few of the shady boys working a scam or a con

job. But the average rural swapper will never meet one of these jaspers in his or her lifetime. Neighbors, friends, some people over the ridge or in the next county will be your trading partners, the people Thomas Jefferson described as "the small landholders [who] are the most precious part of a state. . . ."

Yet clearly some people are better barterers than others; they shoot the breeze, crack a joke, gossip, and strike a deal with ease while others of us silently rehearse our lines before nervously quavering to a pro-

---

COUNTRY STORE BARTER

In the last century the country store was the neighborhood barter center. Kids brought eggs and poultry they had raised themselves to trade for guns, toys, traps, books; farm women brought fresh-made butter weekly in swap for needed household goods; men brought in furs, hides, butchered stock, and dozens of other farm-raised produce. All country swappers feel a twinge of loss over the disappearance of the trading rural store. But hallelujah! They're not quite dead.

A woman in Mammoth Spring, Arkansas, wrote:

"We moved here to Arkansas recently with very little money, so to help us get started, I've begun to learn the art of 'horse-trading.' . . . We've also found that our local country stores are good places to barter. They're still willing to trade for eggs or a few hours' work . . . and many of the small places use wood-burning stoves for heat, and will swap goods for firewood."

Ask at your country store about barter possibilities—you may be surprised. If you have a garden surplus at harvest time, offer to swap at your nearest co-op. Many country gardeners swap extra cukes, pumpkins, onions, and even zucchini for the rice, lentils, soy flour, wheat germ, and oatmeal they don't grow themselves. ✤

spective swapping partner, "What'll you take for a pound of that fresh spinach?"

There *are* differences in people's bartering abilities; some are differences of personality, others differences in approach and timing. Although there are "born traders," most of us can learn to be good at barter with a little practice and training in recognizing an opportunity. Remember that "good" barterers are good for different reasons. Two people with radically different approaches to a swapping situation may come out with similar results. If you have something really fine to swap, like a bushel of ripe peaches and a quart of Jersey cream, you can have cloven hooves and neon eyes and still strike a good trade.

A rural community is an interdependent ecosystem where each person or family is linked to the soil, water, topography, crops, weather, and to each other by their own needs, skills, behavior, responses, and demands. Through barter it's possible to identify your own economic role in your neighborhood. You may be the major source of firewood, or have the earliest peas; your knowledge of cows or cars, of cabbages or cranberries may make you indispensable in the community. Take a fresh look at yourself and your neighbors. See who is putting what into the community, and who is taking what out of it.

There are no specific lists of qualities identifying a good trader. Every personal and local situation is unique and has to be worked out by participant swappers. It's easier to list the possibilities for barter that exist, ways to ease into barter situations, and, gradually, how to swap instead of spend. It takes a while to get into a bartering way of life, but the less money you use and need, the more resourceful you will become. The more you barter, the more comfortable you will be with this way of living. The ideal to aim for is a *voluntary low cash income.* R.E. Gould, the Yankee storekeeper *par excellence,* once asked an old barter-

"You can read me the poem *after* I plow your garden."

ing farmer how much money he needed each year for "extras."

He said he needed one dollar to subscribe to the paper and a little for postage and a few things like that. After figuring a few minutes he concluded, "I can get by with seven dollars, but I had ought to have eleven."

He swapped and bartered for the rest of life's necessities.

Greasing the Skids

Old-timers who had to move heavy logs or rocks or machinery knew they could handle ponderous weights more easily by smearing axle grease on the skid logs. Swappers have developed their own kind of axle grease, largely dictated by common sense.

People who swap often are sensitive to others' needs, offers, and personalities. They listen and look, rather than overwhelming a barter prospect with a barrage of glib verbosity.

Swappers learn to be inventive and ingenious. Out of a tangled net of impossibilities or an apparently inactive situation they can pull out a good trade. One of the best swapping legends involved a smart-aleck storekeeper and a quick-witted Indian who was partial to rum. The storekeeper liked needling teases and practical jokes, and "took" the Indian in a swap for "as much rum as you can carry away in a bushel basket." He had quite a few good laughs describing the Indian's face as he comprehended how he'd been taken. But the smile shifted to the other side of his face one bitterly cold February day when the Indian stalked into the store with a bushel basket that had been dipped several times in water and was thickly coated with a layer of ice, and said, "Fill it up with my rum."

Another inventive swapper was the well-dressed but grossly overweight Texan who reduced from 287 pounds to a slim 160. Most people would have delighted in heaving the expensive jumbo-sized suits and shirts out the door, but not this trader. He searched until he found a fat farmer, then swapped some of the XXL garments for a season's supply of fresh vegetables. Not content, he then sought out an overweight tax accountant and traded him a $200 suit for three years' tax work.

In some states, hunters who do not own land face a long series of dreary rounds, asking for permission to hunt on private land. For the most part the answers are negative scowls. But two bartering hunters with wide-awake swapping instincts offered the owners of a secluded cabin in the Virginia mountains, people who had never allowed any gunners on their land before, a swap they couldn't resist. In return for hunting privileges, they built the owners a handsome porch on the cabin out of aged barn timbers owned by one of the hunters. The swap grew, as many swaps do, into a custom, and next spring the hunters were back with their fly rods, trading their labor in cabin repairs for a few hours on the stream.

Good traders often include a little bonus in a swap. If they are trading organic vegetables, they throw in a bunch of dried flowers or a comb of honey; if they're trading the loan of a tractor over the weekend, they give Friday afternoon or Monday morning extra; if they're trading canning jars, they'll add a quart or two of something special already put up. This kind of dividend swapping not only sweetens the pot, but creates good will and eager swapping partners in the future.

Country swappers keep up on things, looking for all possible chances to barter. They know what parcels of land are up for sale, who's got new calves, what dogs have had puppies, whose hay rake is broken, who just got fifty pounds of prunes from Uncle Jack in California. The next step is to ask, "What'll you take for that runty little pup?"

The busiest swappers are those who trade fair and square, who know that the best deal is the one where everybody involved in the swap is pleased. R.E. Gould used to describe the running swap battles between his father and a slippery old Maine trader known as Horace-by-God, as a long series of "laying traps" and evening up the scores on evil trades. While these Yankee reminiscences make good reading and better stove-side tales, they're not much fun when you're on the short end of a sharp trader's stick in real life.

Barter for Profit

Most of the swaps described so far have been even-steven, one-to-one barters among neighbors and friends—the easiest, most simple and satisfying trades. But some people barter for profit, and a few make a good living that way on an absolute minimum of cash. The intensity and the style of barter for profit can vary enormously, from local "horse trading" to international barter empires masterminded by men who make *Catch-22*'s Milo Minderbinder look retarded. Here are some common barter-for-profit techniques.

Trading Up

This technique involves not just swapping something you've got for something you want, but trading

whatever you've got for something of *greater value* every time you swap. Every time. This is "trading up" or "pyramiding." Barter lore is rich in these ladder-swap success stories, like Gould's description in *Yankee Drummer* of the Maine man who went to a fair and at the day's end reported: "Had a good day. I've traded horses eleven times and now I have a better horse than I started with, $14 in cash, a grindstone, a setting hen, and a bushel of beans." He had traded up nobly.

To trade up takes considerable knowledge of market values in the commodities you're dealing with as well as a truly businesslike attitude. It takes having resources and the resilient attitude to absorb a loss from time to time. It takes the ability to recognize a possible deal, to examine everyone you meet with a speculative eye. It takes hard work and unremitting hustling, whether you're trading gold, real estate, wheat futures, or the cuckoo clocks you carved last winter.

"Horse traders," as small-scale profit barterers are called, often have a swapping fever that burns inside them, keeping them pyramiding their gains and working deals. Every encounter offers opportunities, a chance to win. Trading is not only a way to earn a living, but a fascinating, compelling game. Many of these professional traders cultivate eccentric ways, dress oddly, and work at being characters. Their yards and barns tend to be a mad jumble of chairs, bird baths, used tractors, empty bottles, parts of cars, horseshoes, sundials, rusty bicycles, church steeples, bird cages, and rolls of fencing, a disorderly confusion that lures many people to it with its promise of possible valuable antiques waiting to be discovered.

THE HORSE TRADER'S HANDBOOK

1. *Know the current market values of everything.* Keep some up-to-date catalogs in the back room—Sears' mail order catalog, a farm supply catalog, an antiques price guide, and an automotive parts price guide are indispensable. When a prospect brings in Granny's butter churn to swap, just make an excuse to duck out for a minute, run to your catalog library, and see what butter churns are bringing on the antique market.

2. *Know the wants of the community.* If you remember that the Hellesponts got a Jersey cow a month ago, then you can guess they're about ready to kill for a butter churn. You might be able to swap this one for one of those registered Collie pups they've got.

3. *Trade for anything that comes along.* You can never tell when you might need a square of shingles, a road grader, a

pair of chore boots, a mushroom guide, or 4,000 meerschaum pipes to clinch a deal.

4. *Only swap UP.* If you can't make a profit, let the deal go. Someone else will come along.

5. *Size up your barter prospect.* Talk for a while—get an idea of the other person's character, weaknesses, swapping expertise, and greed. Notice the pipe he's smoking—maybe he'd like 4,000 meerschaums.

6. *Make the swap sound complex.* Dazzle the other fellow with details and numbers so he can hardly follow you. Make it sound like *he's* getting the best of a big deal—shake your head ruefully and tsk-tsk that he's too smart for you, while practicing Rule 4.

7. *Get him to name a value first.* This puts him on the defensive and sticks him with a stated value while you are free to register incredulity, to laugh, story tell, and counter-offer at will.

8. *Keep 'em off balance.* Dress "pore," play the character, talk like one. If you keep them entertained, you may distract them from hard bargaining.

9. *Sweeten the pot.* If the prospect has brought kids along, give them each a lollipop and a grin. Now the parents feel obligated to you and you haven't even started to dicker.

* * *

The horse trader often dresses in stained and ragged clothes. This is a clever psychological ploy that gives him a subtle advantage in a barter deal; his better-dressed opponent feels both ill at ease and somehow superior. He or she is less inclined to stoop to the ragged trader's level of intense bartering. Somewhat off balance, distracted from the finer points of the haggle by the trader's odd appearance and sometimes behavior which can range from tobacco chewing to a weird laugh, the amateur swapper rarely comes out of the deal ahead.

Other traders depend on vociferous enthusiasm and a string of jokes and stories to get the prospects worked up. Eloquent and persuasive, they both charm and amuse the flies that walk into their webs. A common trick is to bury the prospective swapper under a confusing landslide trade offer involving multiple items: "Tell you what I'll do, I'll let you have this nice pair of antique plates, two bales of wool remnants, this box of plant holders and a set of dominoes for your old brass bed. You won't do better than that anywhere!"

Multiple Swaps

Complex trades involving three or more people, all "controlled" by the initiating swapper, can realize a tidy profit. To handle multiple swaps consistently a barterer has to be part diplomat, have a superb memory, be more than ordinarily astute in recognizing or creating possible trades, and have the ability to pull all the complicated strings that make the trades work out to everyone's satisfaction. Multiple swap trading takes a special kind of person, a wheeler-dealer, a "swappin' fool" like the famous Jack Redshaw, the King of Swap. (Big business bartering has more nobility than the British House of Lords. There are various Barter Barons, a Barter King or two, and several Princes of Swap.) From humble beginnings Jack swapped up through stickpins and watches to fabulous jewels, Liberian tankers, Bolivian streetcars, and racehorses.

Charles Wilson, in his *Let's Try Barter*, describes one of the typical Redshaw barter deals. It involved Redshaw, a farm-owning college professor with two daughters, a local banker, and a local farmer. The college professor inherited a huge bank vault. He couldn't use it and he couldn't sell it. He approached Redshaw with his plaint, and it was disclosed that each daughter

DON'T INSULT ME BY OFFERING MONEY (EYUCK!)

yearned for her own gentle horse to ride. Redshaw had
no prospect in mind for the bank vault, but he knew of
a local farmer who wanted to get rid of two complacent
saddle horses that were eating him into the poorhouse,
so he swapped a couple of stuffed chairs from his vast
inventory to the farmer for the horses, then swapped
the horses for the bank vault. The vault sat for a while
awaiting the right moment, which arrived in the form
of a local banker who took the vault and gave Redshaw
a one-carat diamond ring, two shotguns, ". . . and $300
in loathsome cash."

As Trader Jack's reputation grew, the deals came to
him through the door and through the mail—corncob
pipes, carousels, rubies, salted fish, Chinese jade—
everything.

Almost every rural area has a Trader Jack in miniature, and such an energetic person can keep the community distribution of goods rotating and lively. The real Trader Jack was shrewd and well-informed on the current market values of hundreds of items from crystal chandeliers to antique steam engines. He concealed some of his sharp expertise behind a down-home, affable, rural-talkin' exterior. He knew the value of long-range plans in multiple barter, and had no hesitation in swapping for a good bargain he didn't need at the moment, then holding it for future speculation.

Triangulation

Triangulation is a multiple swap. Many times a simple one-to-one swap won't work. You have a huge gardenful of broccoli to swap and you're looking for a solar panel to rig up a hot water system. You know of a woman, Ramona, who has an extra solar panel left over from her greenhouse project, but when you approach her about a possible swap she says she loathes broccoli, good-by. The simple swap has failed. A little digging on your part turns up Signora Pittora, who runs an Italian restaurant in a nearby town. The Signora is delighted to find a good source of fresh, succulent broccoli and offers to barter free lunches for the green vegetable. But what you want is a solar panel, not dining out. Back you go to Ramona, and you discover that she adores eating out and would be delighted with lunches at Signora Pittora's restaurant as long as she isn't served broccoli. The arrangement is made for the three-way deal: the Signora gets your broccoli, Ramona gets the lunches and you get the solar panel—triangulation has solved the problem of a stuck swap.

Triangulation is a common barter device. It is the hinge that allows barter clubs and groups to function,

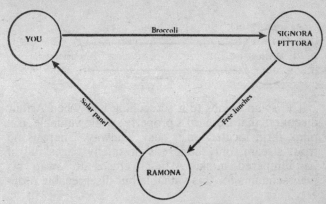

and that gives them their *raison d'être,* for one-to-one swaps that satisfy both parties are hard for individual barterers to track down much of the time.

Vehicles

Sometimes even a multiple or triangular swap gets stuck in the middle. Negotiations come to a dead halt because one of the items involved in the trade is not wanted by one of the swappers—either he doesn't need it or he thinks his chances of passing it on in another swap are dim. A "vehicle" can save the day.

Vehicles are literally something that gets the deal moving from one swapper to another, and are usually objects that are always desirable, easy to trade, like gold and silver coins or precious gems, which are portable and have recognized value everywhere.

For example: Arthur has 4,000 meerschaum pipes that he wishes to swap for a piece of property with a trout stream where he can build a log cabin and spend his retirement years presenting dry flies to wily trout. Someone has put him in touch with Bernard, who wants to open a pipe and cigar mail order business and has a piece of property that he wants to swap for shop stock, such as meerschaum pipes. So far the deal looks good. A straight swap of pipes for property.

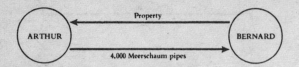

The swap comes to a screeching halt when Arthur discovers that Bernard's property, while valuable, is a mink farm located on a busy highway. There is no trout stream, only hundreds of smelly cages full of bad-tempered mink. Arthur refuses to swap his meerschaums for this valuable but disagreeable property.

Bernard is in despair, and so is Arthur—until Clara comes onto the scene. Clara is a fur designer. Bernard meets her at his sister's wedding, and with an experienced swapper's eye for possibilities, discovers that Clara craves her own mink farm as a dependable source of inexpensive furs. Clara has a *vehicle* in the form of two diamonds of excellent quality that she wants to swap for the mink farm. Bernard whispers in Arthur's ear and is delighted to find that Arthur is only too willing to accept diamonds which he thinks will appreciate rapidly in value and are highly negotiable. The deal is now the familiar triangle:

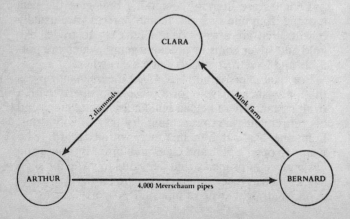

The diamonds have the swap moving again after the stalemate. Yet Arthur still does not have his retirement place, only the two diamonds. But he accepted the jewels precisely because they are desirable and easily traded, so he is quickly able to find his dream property through a real estate trader who likes the portability, security, and upward valuation of diamonds.

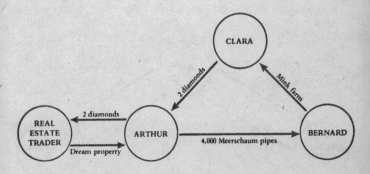

But gemstones and gold coins are as rare as hen's teeth in rural communities. Nonetheless, trading vehicles do exist, though of a different sort. Seasoned hardwood is an excellent country barter vehicle—even if you can't use it yourself, plenty of people want and need it. So are maple syrup, sorghum, sides of beef or pork, fat turkeys. Look at your own community area to see what everyone agrees is a valuable commodity, and consider its possibilities as a barter vehicle.

Car mechanic Ace makes house calls and repairs everything from sports cars to hay balers. He is also a vegetarian, but has no time to raise a garden. While many of his customers are glad to swap a peck of potatoes or ten pounds of squash when they have a surplus, he wants a steady and ample supply of organically grown vegetables, including eggplant, endive, sorrel, shallots, bok choi, and other delicacies not normally found in average country gardens. The finest organic gardener in Ace's region rides a bicycle, doesn't own a car, and has no use for Ace's services. This gardener, however, is very fond of juicy steaks and sizzling spareribs. Here's how Ace used a side of beef as a vehicle:

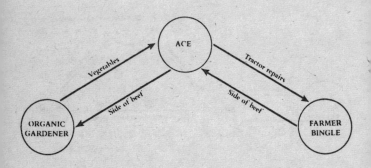

Value Increase Over Time

Barterers for profit often swap for land, gold, gemstones, fine wine, engraved guns, master paintings, fine old furniture, and other rare or limited edition objects that *increase in value over time*. Anything rare and beautiful will appreciate over time. Investors in fine art try to guess who the Picassos and Homers of the future will be. Land traders try to guess which way development is moving.

For example, rural and small town land and houses are choice properties now, and their value is increasing annually. The value of choice rural property has increased over the past ten years so briskly that it has outstripped inflation! Professional land investors name an annual 10 percent appreciation for farm and rural properties in this period. City slicker businessmen invest in farms because of the lure of substantial tax advantages. European investors have been eyeing and buying American rural property for some time.

Financial expert Howard Ruff advises in his *How to Prosper During the Coming Bad Years:*

> I believe that almost any small town in America . . . that does not have a large welfare population, is going to boom. If it is surrounded by diversified agriculture and not dependent on one big industry or plant, it's even better. Many smaller communities are adopting aggressive "no growth" policies, which means that they cannot easily increase the supply of existing housing. This increases the value of available property. Almost any land near the small towns will appreciate.
>
> . . . Sell (or trade) all big city or suburban real estate and invest in small town income property. Move if possible.

Ruff's recommendations are based on his belief that the current inflationary spiral will end in an "economic smash-up" that sees big cities going bankrupt and the middle-class and affluent people who are able to escape the crash moving into the small towns and countryside in a flood. Those who look ahead and make their moves before the fall will control the property that will suddenly leap in value.

Land is only one example of a value increase over time. It is in natural limited supply. Erosion, poor agricultural practices, highways, population expansion, parking lots, cemeteries all decrease the real amount of land. Diamonds also appreciate over time, not because the supply is finite, but because it is controlled by the De Beers diamond cartel, which allows diamonds only to trickle onto the market. Diamond prices are remarkable because they rarely fall. Yet rural barterers with an eye to profit can find a few rough diamonds that become steadily more valuable as the years pass. Old farm implements, antique woodworking tools, heirloom furniture, old family china and silver, the clock on the mantle, all are "collectibles" or antiques that appreciate over time. The swapper or collector expects to hold onto such objects, sometimes for years, before trying to barter them. It is a patient, waiting game.

Creative Barter

Land, diamonds, antiques—they're out of reach of most country people who have neither the time nor the inclination for speculative bartering. But more homely items increase in value over time. Baby pigs grow into big pork roasts, hams, and bacon; calves grow into steaks; baby chicks grow into egg-layers; a few packets of garden seed mature in a season into a bountiful

harvest; apple whips grow into orchards; young trees become marketable timber. All of these are *creative value increases,* and they are within the reach of almost every rural person. The surpluses are a real kind of wealth that can be efficiently bartered locally without ever resorting to far-away markets, banks, and the bother of cash money, checks, or tedious paperwork. Direct barter based on the surplus resulting from these creative value increases is more efficient than converting your surplus to money that you then spend for what you need.

Jack and Jasmine are hard-working but unimaginative homesteaders whose thinking patterns are tediously locked into money, checks, record-keeping, banks, loans, budgets, and dollar prices. They moved to the country with a vague idea of self-sufficiency and supplying all their needs with their own hands. The ideal faded quickly as they discovered they had neither the time nor the skill to make shoes, window glass, nails, faucets, a hot water heater, needles, barrels, buckets, ropes, ink, books, papers, and a thousand other things. They also needed cash money for gasoline, farming equipment, telephone, electricity, taxes, and transportation.

Because they had never bartered they saw that they had no choice but to get their hands on some cash. They figured they could barely scrape by with $10,000 annually, and set out to make it on their homestead farm. Jack specialized in growing asparagus as a money crop while Jasmine made delicate decorative baskets of wild materials. Jack spent a lot of time in his labor-intensive asparagus beds, but even more time on the telephone setting up deals with produce managers in grocery markets. When the asparagus season came he drove back and forth between the city and his farm delivering asparagus three times a week. First the asparagus had to be cut, bunched, tied, and packed, and the long trips took time and gas. In the second season Jack switched to a wholesaler who bought and picked up Jack's whole harvest, but at a depressingly low price. When Jack complained, the wholesaler pointed out that he was in competition with California agribusiness asparagus growers, and he should be glad to get the price he did.

Jasmine's baskets were beautiful but hard to move. She took them into the city and tried to interest buyers in gift shops and department stores. The city was full of Far Eastern imported baskets at prices far cheaper than Jasmine could make hers, and she ended up placing the baskets in eleven shops on consignment. The record-keeping was a headache, and she had to check back every month or so with each shop. At the end of the second year Jack and Jasmine had made $10,000, but it had been an exhausting, full-time hassle, with a lot of travel and phone calls.

Because they buy everything, their $10,000 doesn't go far, and they do without many of the little grace-

"We need more
wine. Got any
more broccoli?"

"There's two bunches
in my pocketbook."

notes of life that make the difference between exis-
tence and pleasant living. The bookkeeping takes them
a full morning once a week. They pay income taxes on
the $10,000. It seems a hard way to make a living, and
now Jack and Jasmine say that the small farmer hasn't
got a chance these days.

Billy and Babes also have a small farm not far from
Jack. They grew up in the country and are natural and
confirmed barterers. They figure that the lowest
amount of cash they need to get by is $3,500 a year for
taxes, phone, electricity, gas, and a few other non-
barterable materials. Everything else they will swap
for locally. Billy's cash crops are Christmas trees and
strawberries. Both are pick-your-own crops, so he has
no transportation, cutting, picking, or packing costs,
no wasted days hustling them in urban areas. For local

barter Billy cuts firewood from his managed woodlot and also makes maple syrup—one a necessity, the other a luxury, both from his maple woods. With these products he can swap for auto repairs, shoes, clothing, building materials, anything made or sold locally. Many of his "customers" depend on him to keep them in syrup and wood. Billy and Babes tend the big garden and orchard. In the fall they swap eating apples and cider for a neighbor's smoked bacon, another neighbor's butchered lamb, pork, and beef. At the annual church swap festival Babes trades giant show pumpkins for potatoes, turnips, crocks of sauerkraut, fruit cake, jam, jellies, and pickles. Like Jasmine, Babes also makes baskets. But hers are big, sturdy splint laundry baskets, practical, long-lasting, and handsome, of a kind impossible to find in the stores. Babes doesn't take these around to shops; she puts a sign on the lawn and an ad in the paper. The quality of the baskets is so good and their function so useful that word of mouth brings her more customers than she can comfortably handle. She barters or takes cash for the baskets and keeps the family supplied with everything from comforters and fishing tackle to hand-knit sweaters. At the end of the year Billy and Babes have gotten by on only $3,500; their paperwork has been minimal. They are well fed, comfortable, and their lives are satisfying. They think that a small farm is the ideal way to make a living. For them it is.

CHAPTER 4

Group Barter

Although barter is the natural economy of the rural world, in the generations since World War II, radio, television, and cars have fostered urban values and made them familiar and even tantalizing to many country people. The population move from city to country has brought a wave of new people with different ideas and different ways into the small towns and farm communities. These people have no experience with barter and its techniques and are not used to the slower rhythms of country trading. In many places the close-knit fabric of traditional rural exchange has disintegrated.

You may *want* to barter, but be reluctant to begin. It's easier and faster to let money talk for us than to negotiate on a personal level, especially if your attention is focused on accumulating goods rather than living a simpler life. You may *need* to barter, but not know where or how to find a fellow swapper who has what you want and who wants what you have. You may *have* to barter, but resent the amount of time you spend tracking down trades. The bartering habits of your community may have fallen into disuse, with no one quite sure how to start them up again.

All of these problems can be solved by non-profit community barter organizations that can range in size from a loose association of four or five cooperative neighborhood families to a well-organized and tightly run skillsbank with hundreds of members.

Direct Exchange

Direct exchange groups have a central record system, no matter how simple, and function as a clearinghouse to pair off swappers who are looking for each other. This record system can be as uncomplicated as a bulletin board in a public place where prospective swappers post their "haves" and look for what they need.

A bulletin board setup must have dated notices that don't stay over-long, and it's helpful if the space is broken down into columns headed up with permanent category markers such as: Labor, Arts and Crafts, Farm Help, Livestock, Housing, Mechanical and Electrical, Transportation, Health, Children. Participants put up their own cards, and the responsibility for finding a swap partner is on the individual. Some organized centers use the bulletin board format, although it is in an office and attended by a director or staff. Organized centers usually have a formal list of members, each of whom pays a fee to the barter center. This covers mailing costs, office rent, paper and supplies, and perhaps a director's salary.

More effective is the direct barter exchange that puts out a bulletin, quarterly or more often. The bulletin replaces the bulletin board, and is a booklet listing members' haves and wants in categories. This has several advantages. Members can study them in the comfort and calmness of home instead of standing in front of a bulletin board scribbling notes on the back of an envelope. Non-members may see them and be attracted to the barter organization. They are a convenience for people with transportation problems or handicaps who find it a nuisance to get to a central bulletin board.

The Green Thumb Barter Band is a fictional example of a direct exchange group in a semi-rural area. It is an organization of serious and amateur gardeners who have discovered that swapping equipment, skills, machinery, space, plant cuttings and seedlings, practical information, and harvest produce is more satisfying than buying. Because the members' interests are focused around horticulture and agriculture, direct exchanges are easy to work out.

The Green Thumb Band has a central "office" which is the rolltop desk near a phone in the founding member's big farm kitchen. A cross-referenced box of file cards lists members, their skills and specialties, their "gives" and "takes." It is the heart of the system.

GREEN THUMB BARTER BAND
MEMBER CARD

Name: Frances Frill (Mrs.) phone: 444-4444
Old State Road, Mineshaft, MI

Specialties: tomatoes, herbs, rock gardens

Expertise: 5 blue ribbons County Fair for
tomatoes

Equipment: hand tools, garden cart

Have: tomato seedlings, will grow on shares;
rock garden design and plants

Needs: greenhouse space, rototilling, manure,
bu. baskets

Notes: works at hospital Mon.–Wed.

Twice a year the Green Thumb puts out its small mimeographed bulletin listing the possible swaps. Each member pays a small fee for the listing to cover the bulletin's production and distribution costs. Each member must make the contact with the desired swapping partner and establish the values of the items traded. The system works fairly smoothly and is somewhat self-regulating in terms of supply and demand. The coordinator, a busy orchard owner, takes his "pay" for keeping the rolltop desk operating by getting a little produce or labor from each member. Here is a typical listing page from the spring bulletin.

HAVES	WANTS
will prune fruit trees	experienced estate gardener
native woodland ferns	imported Dutch tulip bulbs
100 back issues *Horticulture*	hardy table grape cuttings
cabbage sets—8 different varieties	help designing a water garden
greenhouse space	Big Boy tomato sets
weekday use my rototiller	used garden tools
will weed gardens after school	clay pots—large sizes only
vegetable seeds—lg. assortment	Saturday morning garden help
sign up now for muskmelon shares!	manure, delivered
have good garden plot	ticket to N.Y. Flower Show
sharecrop cherry trees	orchid growing information
African violets	paving stones for garden walk
information on dye plants and flax growing	old gardening books
tomato stakes and garden fencing	European lettuce varieties seeds

Mrs. Frill, the prize-winning tomato grower, has listed her need for Big Boy tomato sets. She lives in a trailer with no room to start seeds indoors. No one seems to be starting Big Boys this year. But when she notices that a fellow member is offering greenhouse space, she calls, rearranges her priorities, and starts her own Big Boy seeds in Mr. Gerbil's greenhouse. In exchange he takes a bushel of the big, luscious fruits at harvest time.

A simple, small-scale direct exchange group like the Green Thumb Barter Band is not hard to get started, especially when it's possible to focus on a restricted membership like the horticulturally minded members of the Green Thumb. Other groups can concentrate on exchanging general skills, on providing transportation or baby-sitting services, can relate to neighbors swapping chores, or vacationers swapping houses. A direct exchange group could be an emotional support group whose members trade compassion and understanding and provide on-call support for each other, or it could be a swappers' brain trust exchanging such esoteric skills as instruction in Urdu, calculus, writing Latin prose, map-making, or practical solar technology. The scope is as vast as human experience, and the groups as flexible as humans themselves.

A good way to start a small country swap group is with your nearest neighbors. Talk to five or six families who live along your road. Discover what skills and abilities can go into your trading bank; find out who is willing to swap time and equipment rather than spend money. Remember, if your neighbors have a new tractor or brushcutter, they may be reluctant to loan it out, but would feel fine about running the equipment themselves in trade for something needed.

Find out what the biggest common need is among you and your neighbors—seasonal labor, use of machinery and equipment, dependable transportation, neighborly contact, or agricultural or livestock skills, and base your first swaps on these needs. A natural

expansion will follow successful swaps. After you've talked to everybody, get them all together; it's important that you all know each other. After all, you're neighbors, aren't you? Have a potluck supper to which everyone contributes, itself a kind of swapping.

Here's a brief list of questions that will gauge your own and your neighbors' swap consciousness.

☞ Has the pinch of inflation shriveled your spending dollars to the point where you worry about making ends meet? Does the thought of expensive gas and travel wear and tear on your vehicle make you hesitate before you drive into town for needed parts or supplies?

☞ Do you have any clothing, equipment, or machinery that you no longer use but that still has plenty of good wear in it? Would you consider swapping these items instead of storing them or throwing them away?

☞ Have you ever done any trading or swapping before? What was it and how did the swap turn out?

☞ Have you ever thought how much easier life would be if the old-time work parties like barn raisings and bridge building still went on?

☞ If there's something you really have to have, like a new chain saw bar, a set of snow tires, or storm windows, and you're down to the bottom of your sock, do you usually buy it on time, go without, or borrow the money to pay for it? How would you like to swap for it?

Even in a small neighbors' exchange group some kind of organization is helpful. It need not be as elaborate as the rolltop desk "office" of the Green Thumb Barter Band, but there should be a record of the simple rules you all decide on, the direction the barter should take, and what should happen in case of dispute. The chairmanship of the group can rotate, thus sharing the responsibility for central coordination. It's a good idea to get together every few weeks for a work party or common dinner to keep communication flowing.

Parity, or judging the values of different people's time and equipment, is not always simple. Some barter groups, especially those looking for an alternative economic system, say everyone's time is equally valuable, be it doctor, lawyer, stable hand, wood chopper, car mechanic, farrier, physicist, seamstress, or carpet-installer. Such an equal division can work well in rural barter where experience and hard work can count for as much if not more than advanced education and esoteric skills.

But suppose you own a backhoe, and have been called on by every member of the group to do an hour's work here, or a morning's labor there with your machine. Does an hour's work splitting wood by hand by your neighbor Willy equal your hour's work with your backhoe on his new stock pond? Not likely, for you're still paying off that backhoe with cash and it gobbles gas like there's no tomorrow. You and Willy agree to relative values—say, three of his hours with his axe to one of yours with the heavy equipment, or you set up "hour values" based on the current market dollar values of wood-splitting and backhoe operation.

Again, Mary Vanilla is another neighbor, and she is a skilled seamstress. She can make a wool suit that is the equal in quality of anything from an exclusive shop. You also sew, but anything more complex than a straight seam is a challenge. Your work tends to be lumpy and ill-fitting, you use cheap synthetic fabrics and cutesy-poo patterns with big-eyed doggies all over the place. Is an hour of your sewing time equal to an hour of Mary's? No way. Mary's *skill* makes her time more valuable than yours. Just *how* valuable will have to be worked out by the group. Nor does this mean that there is no barter market for your sewing skills; let Mary tailor the fancy suits and jackets—you can sew sturdy and useful pot holders, hem tablecloths, and work up dozens of simpler but needed objects.

So, these are the three basic approaches to parity.

- Everybody's labor/time is equally valuable.

- Skilled labor has greater value than unskilled.

- Value of members' work is established by translating current market dollar values into barter time.

In the country there is an important exception to the belief that skilled labor has greater intrinsic value than unskilled labor, and that is when the product of the unskilled labor is a necessity of life, and that of the skilled labor is not. For example, Dr. Zip is a cosmetic plastic surgeon who lives in the country. He is well educated and highly skilled. Woodcutter Joe is

neither. Yet, if Dr. Zip wants to be warm in an arctic winter, he may swap his surgical skills for seasoned cordwood at par or less value than Joe's apparent market rate. Because Joe deals in an essential commodity (firewood) he can get his squashed nose re-made (a non-essential service) for a fraction of what Zip usually gets for his skilled services.

WHY AN INFORMAL NEIGHBOR SWAP GROUP HELPS EVERYONE

☛ The increased sense of solidarity, strength, and support you get from knowing you have dependable, responsible neighbors who will help out when help is needed.

☛ Everybody saves cash money, time, and worry. Because the swapping is between nearby neighbors, transportation expenses, one of the problems of rural living, are nil.

☛ The regular chores and tasks of country living become easier when shared. There is truth in the adage, "Many hands make light work."

Indirect Exchange

A barter group larger than a few neighbors or a group with more varied interests than the Green Thumb Barter Band will find direct exchange difficult or restrictive in many cases. A wider range of interests and skills means more complex swaps, triangulation, and vehicles to ease balked barter. For example, Mrs. Frill may want to swap her tomatoes for a course of Swedish massages or a weekend in Montreal or instruction in sailing—all beyond the abilities of the Green Thumb Band members. Membership in an indirect exchange group can help her.

Indirect exchanges work something like banks: your skills and goods and labor earn you *credits* within the membership. When you use someone else's labor or skills, they get the credits and your account is *debited*. The larger the group the more varied the skills and abilities of the membership and the more attractive the range of barter possibilities.

Some organizations issue "check books" or "credit cards" to members, and send them monthly statements of their barter credits or debits. Others keep only central records. The ideal is to maintain a good balance between your barter credits and debits, neither amassing so many credits for your input that you have difficulty "spending" them, nor using the services of others so freely without reciprocating that you are saddled with large debits.

Obviously a barter group organized around indirect exchange must have a central office and a fairly sophisticated system of keeping records of the credits and debits of each member. This means regular statements, bookkeeping personnel, phone expenses, office space, printing costs, mailing costs, postage, and staff salaries. It is standard for members of an indirect exchange to pay fees *in money* to keep the center rolling smoothly. (Profit barter clubs, which are indirect exchanges, charge an annual membership fee, often several hundred dollars, and a percentage on every barter transaction.) Office workers are generally paid cash salaries, though some organizations pay partly in cash and partly in barter.

Doug Bradley of Madison, Wisconsin, founder of SWAP (Sharing Work and Products), a non-profit barter center with 190 members, remarks in the newsletter, *Exchange Networks,*

> . . . Should the center be simply a passive broker, linking individuals and other organizations who have something to offer with those who are requesting it (and vice versa) or should the center itself be actively involved in bartering with its membership (i.e., for office help, rent, printing, etc.)?

SWAP was able to talk a neighborhood association, Neighborhood House, into trading office space with lights, heat, and other utilities in return for ". . . telephone answering service, a Christmas tree and lights, a Ping Pong table, occasional maintenance services, outreach coordination, and most importantly, articles and technical assistance for the Neighborhood House bimonthly publication, *The Neighborhood House News.*" SWAP recommends that other non-profit barter groups establish similar barter relationships with established community, religious, or neighborhood organizations.

These larger, more complex groups need considerably more management than the easygoing little direct exchange groups. Organization is important, and the more successful groups have a board of governors, a director, clearly outlined jobs and responsibilities, an office staff, incorporation articles, rules and bylaws. Funding—from government, state, civic, or private sources or through the membership—is vital to get these big birds off the ground. A large membership has to be built up. This kind of organization is far more common in urban or suburban settings than in the country where neither the formality of organization, the requisite membership numbers, nor the nonessential nature of many of the skills and goods listed in city directories is possible. There are still tremendous differences between what city and country people deem important. The following offers are taken from an urban barter bulletin; there would be few takers in a rural farm community.

bartending	juggling
grant writing	repairing plaster statues
public relations work	tipi construction
bead rings	advice on fasting
astrology charts	makeup tips
Fortran programming	tennis partner
penny whistle lessons	karate

These offers would find takers quickly:

manure spreading	baled hay
will electrify barns	weekend dairy farm work
pigs castrated	wanted
grazing meadow	woodlot management
bred Toggenberg goats	horse harness, new and
used farm machinery	used
fence work	water dowsing

The rural swapper who yearns for instruction in dulcimer making or T'ai Chi or disco dancing lessons, will find a ready and enthusiastic acceptance of his or her surplus country products when contacts are made with a town or city barter group. If you feel there's more to life than a full woodshed, a well-lined pantry, and the chores all done, look around for a nearby large-scale exchange group. If you think there are enough people like you in your area, you might want to try starting a local wide-interest exchange group.

Starting an Exchange

Professor Ted Shannon of the University of Wisconsin Extension Service, long concerned with underemployment and wasted skills in the American population, in 1977 undertook an examination of barter and the economic possibilities it offered. A publication resulted from Shannon's barter research and experimentation. It is called the *Barter Research Project*. The project itself was a broad examination of barter techniques in the United States and other parts of the world, and from it came practical step-by-step guidelines and advice on starting barter groups. Some of the major guidelines put forth in the publication were condensed by editor Dave Tobin for inclusion in the September-October 1980 issue of *Exchange Networks*. Here are some suggestions from them.

☞ The first step is to define goals and target population. Is it intended to be a total or partial system? Is the project aimed at specific goods, services, and skills, and for what purpose? Who is the target population?

☞ Find some seed money either through existing public or private agencies, foundations, businesses, individuals, or community funds.

☞ Set up an information system. It can be as loose as public announcements on a bulletin board or as tight as a computer readout at the home office. Most exchanges and clearinghouses use a file card system with master cards and skill, goods, services, exchange cards with give/take or credit/debit sections. These cards must have all the basic information needed for the exchange to function—name, address, time to call and phone, zone, date and description of goods, services, and skills needed or available. They must also record the credit value of the exchange and type of exchange. It helps to color-code these cards for quick reference. This will provide an ongoing profile for most research material needed.

☞ Another critical part of making a barter system work is publicity. People have to know what's available and how to get to it. They need to know what to do and where to go. Informal conversations, bulletin boards at shopping centers, and newspaper swap columns may be sufficient for one-shot personal trades, but an effective ongoing exchange system for a community needs an efficient, thorough approach along more formal channels.

☞ Establish a group of competent people to make the system work. They can be paid staff or volunteers. You may also be able to barter with staff needs (i.e., free day care or school tuition for hours worked).

☞ Establish a name for the organization. It should be clear and help define exactly what the service does to avoid confusion among participants.

☞ Incorporate for legal, business, and liability advantages.

☞ Find a base of operation—work space—in an area that is functional to your objective, i.e., close to public transportation, near or in the target community, etc.

☞ There are two major areas for fund-raising,: external and internal. External funds come from foundations, corporations, business, individual philanthropists, and state and federal agencies. Sources of internal funds are memberships (individual or corporate), printed solicitations, gift memberships, sale of promotional goods, speaking honoraria, and special work projects.

Before plunging into organizing a barter group of considerable size and scope, write to the experienced swap centers and information headquarters listed in *Sources* at the back of this book. There are manuals, newsletters, funding aids, and suggestions for nonprofit community barter groups. In a rural area where the population is spread thinly, the best approach may be to tie a new barter group to an already established organization in the community, whether the barter is a transportation exchange, a baby-sitting exchange, a broad-based general trading center, or a skillsbank.

Skillsbanks

Skillsbank is a word that has come out of the barter movement. Basically, a skillsbank is an organization of people with varied talents and skills who swap their *abilities* with each other. "Everybody has a talent someone else needs" is the motto of Work Exchange, Inc., of Milwaukee, Wisconsin, and the motto could hang over the door of every skillsbank.

Skillsbanks can operate as direct or indirect exchanges. Usually they are indirect exchange centers where a central staff keeps track of members' credits and debits in the bank, and solves any problems that come up. Contact among members is made in several ways such as through that old central bulletin board with the different skills posted, through telephone call-ins to the central office which matches the skill needed with a skill offered, or through a skills directory given to each member of the bank.

Skillsbanks are often outgrowths of other community projects or linked to larger organizations—government-funded self-help programs, volunteer organizations, senior citizens' groups, churches, Junior Leagues, community groups such as Kiwanis or Elks and their auxiliaries, university-community projects—though they can and do stand alone. There is a growing interest in skillsbanks, especially in economically depressed neighborhoods where jobs are few and far between. Although they are usually an urban or suburban phenomenon, organized skillsbanks should work in rural communities, particularly where the influx of city or summer people has been too rapid for newcomers to be absorbed into the traditional life of the region. They should be popular, too, in expanding small towns that are midway between the rural hinterlands and the larger towns within driving range. These small towns, with their shopping centers and specialty stores, function as a central market place and usurp business from the more rural areas. Information and detailed manuals on organizing, funding, operating, and joining a skillsbank, drawn from the experiences of dozens of these barter organizations, are available from the sources listed in the back of this book.

Here are a few examples of how skillsbanks can help rural people.

Tom has just spent his last dollar to buy a ramshackle old farmhouse and twenty acres of hardscrabble hill farm a few miles out from the center of Backwoods, a town with a population of less than 2,000. The area is economically depressed. It has no industry except an ax handle factory that employs seven people. A small general store stocks little more than necessities such as milk, bread, catfood, flashlight batteries and such, the items people run out of and don't want to drive miles into the bigger town to get. There is a dwindling number of working farms in the township, and those that remain are mostly worked by older couples. Yet the town has been enjoying a mild boom. Young city couples and singles, like Tom, have been buying up sections of the old family farms and moving in. Most of these newcomers "work out" in Bustleville twenty miles away, commuting back and forth between the nearest employment and their country properties. Some of them have gardens, chickens, and a little livestock.

Tom is different. He's a fully qualified auto mechanic, owns his own tools, and plans to convert the carriage shed of his falling-down farm outbuildings into a garage and make a living in the country. He's noticed with satisfaction that most of the cars, trucks, and tractors around Backwoods look and sound sick. The nearest repair garage is over in Bustleville. So Tom paints a sign that says:

EXPERT AUTO REPAIRS

Trucks & Tractors a Specialty
$8 per hour

In the city Tom got $12 an hour, but here he figures his overhead will be low and he's willing to take less pay for the pleasure of owning his own place, experiencing the wheeling cycle of seasons, and watching the wild geese migrate. He settles back a little anxiously and hopes the business comes soon, for he badly needs the money to repair the old buildings, insulate the drafty house, replace the antique plumbing, rebuild the dilapidated spring house, buy the shingles for a new roof, have the potholed, eroded long driveway bulldozed, and buy a brushcutter to clear away the scraggly willows and brambles that have moved into the neglected pastures. But nobody comes.

Tom doesn't know it, but nobody can afford him, even at his reduced prices, except the Bustleville commuters, and they get their cars fixed not where they live, but where they work—Bustleville. The rest of the community—unemployed, underemployed, farmers—keep their vehicles running with baling wire, home repairs, and prayer. When something really gives out, it is cannibalized for parts and grafted onto another vehicle of the same kind.

Tom gets desperate about the time that a strong wind tears off a corner of his roof. The rain pours in. Tom is at a low point, feeling worthless, isolated, and doomed to the Bustleville hustle. Then a flyer comes in the mail. It says:

> Join your local Skillsbank!
> The Backwoods Work Exchange
> invites you to barter *your*
> abilities for somebody else's!

Tom reads on, half-remembering that the woman at the general store has a sign at one end of the counter reading WORK EXCHANGE, but he never understood what it was about. O.K., he figures, maybe they've got a carpenter who needs a tune-up. Anything's worth a try.

The next day Tom reels away from the Backwoods Work Exchange clutching a Skillsbank Directory, a mimeographed outline of the Exchange's *modus operandi*, a newsletter, and an invitation to a potluck Swap Supper on Friday night. In the directory, with a listing of ninety-seven members in the surrounding area and a thumbnail vignette of each ("Bobo Jenkins plays the harmonica for the square dances and has won prizes for his bantam poultry"), there are many skills divided into the major categories of Odd Jobs, Minor Repairs, Labor, Home Repair, Construction,

Transportation, Sewing, Baking, Cooperage, Garden Services, Tractor Work, Livestock, and dozens of others.

That afternoon Tom starts calling. He finds Maurice, a roofing contractor on weekends (Monday through Friday he works at the ax handle factory), who confesses his truck is almost completely shot. Tom gives it a once-over; Maurice is not just whistling Dixie. The engine needs a complete overhaul, the brakes have to be relined, the shocks must be replaced, and body work is essential if it's going to pass another inspection. It all adds up to a staggering total, even at $8 an hour. Tom and Maurice agree it is about equal to a roofing job for the house.

It turns out that Maurice's brother-in-law Charlie is a carpenter part-time, and has three cars, none of them operative. Charlie has been swapping construction and

repair work for transportation to a part-time job. Tom makes a deal. Charlie will repair those decaying buildings in return for the rejuvenation of two of his defunct cars, but not before Tom swaps a brake job for some rough-cut lumber, a tune-up for ten pounds of nails, and a complicated welding job on the town bulldozer for an hour's work on his bumpy driveway.

Suddenly Tom knows everybody in town, he has all the business he can handle, his property is shaping up fast, a lot of people's vehicles are purring along again, and everybody waves to him when they go by. If Tom had had to ferret out everybody he did business with, it would have taken him years. The Backwoods Work Exchange has saved his bacon, and fast. One of the major advantages of a skillsbank is its ability to make speedy connections between barterers.

Mazie is a different case. She is a 78-year-old widow who has lived all her life in a quiet little seacoast town. She lives on an extremely restricted income, a tiny pension and some Social Security, and is both too shy and too proud to "take charity." Her life is unremitting anxiety. Will she be able to pay the electric bill and the heating bill for the drafty old house? Can she afford a glazier for the broken window pane or must she tape a piece of cardboard over it? Her meals are frugal by necessity, not choice, for when her husband was alive she was a plump, buxom woman who liked a savory, piping supper. She had always set an outstanding table—pumpkin and rhubarb pie, codfish cakes, baked beans, johnnycake, flapjacks laced with maple syrup and swimming in butter, a crispy roast chicken for Sunday dinner, or a roast beef with Yorkshire pudding that would cost her a week's income now.

Down in Mazie's cellar there is a greedy old oil furnace that limps along, gulping expensive oil and grudging every calorie of heat. Mazie is still hale and hearty and would like to get rid of the oil furnace and install cozy wood stoves in her parlor and kitchen. She even has a wood-burning cookstove, but long ago it was converted to gas, and Mazie can't afford to have it restored. There are twelve large rooms in the house, most of them closed off. She is a lonely old lady because most of her friends have died or moved away. One close friend lives twenty-two miles north, but this is the country and there is no public transportation. Mazie has no car, nor can she drive.

One of her passions is gardening, and she has an extensive vegetable garden. She also has a superb rose garden, full of fragrant old-fashioned varieties and several roses unknown beyond the border of her garden, for Mazie is a dedicated rosarian who hybridizes new varieties. She has heritage roses, Damask, Moss, Centifolia, hybrid teas, and twenty gorgeous tree roses flanking the brick walk that winds through her garden. Mazie doesn't know it, because she lives an ingrown, solitary life, but her rose garden is one of the finest in the state, a unique and beautiful creation that has taken her fifty years to build. Like many elderly people, Mazie's skills and knowledge are unrecognized; she is lonely, cold, and hungry, her clothes are threadbare, but she is determined to "make them last" and does without. She feels powerless to change her life in any way and is stoically resigned to waiting out her days in her creaking old house.

One day in early autumn when the wind off the ocean cuts to the bone, two young women knock on Mazie's door. They explain that they are canvassing the town and trying to draw up a list of people's abilities and skills for a local skillsbank. The experience has been an eye-opener, for even this little village has a rich wealth of human talents and resources. As they talk to Mazie they note the large empty rooms, the chilly air, the big kitchen with its old-fashioned pantry.

Barter is something Mazie understands and respects; there is no taint of charity or condescension in a skillsbank.

The two women ask her what skills she would list. "Well, I used to be able to cook plain New England cooking, not fancy foreign stuff—but I had a light hand with pastry and I knew what stuck to the ribs." She adds modestly, as an afterthought, "And I grow roses," gesturing toward the back of her house. One of the young women takes the trouble to walk out back, and she gasps when she sees the pleached walk, the beds and trellis of roses. She recognizes that here is something extraordinary in the way of rose gardens. When they leave, Mazie is enrolled as a member of the new skillsbank.

A year later and Mazie's life is transformed. Two of the downstairs unused rooms have been "rented out" as a lawyer's office suite in trade for a wood-burning/solar heating system. Two upstairs bedrooms have been bartered for repairs, renovations, and wood-splitting. On Friday mornings Mazie's big kitchen turns into *The New England Cooking School—Home-style Down East Cooking*. The tuition is paid in the form of food supplies, handknit sweaters, homespun yardage, custom-tailored garments, a striped cat, scented soap, newfangled kitchen gadgets, transportation to visit her old friend and "around," as well as the intangible benefits of friendship, company, good food, and the warm glow of self-worth that comes with recognized expertise. Mazie's cooking school has attracted the attention of several food authorities, and editors of newspaper food columns have come from the big city to learn her kitchen tricks. Best of all are Mazie's summer "rose days," when rosarians, horticulturists, and amateur and professional rose growers come to tour her garden and talk roses. Rose varieties are swapped, cuttings traded. Life is full of interest, value, and fellowship for Mazie, all directly sprung from the cashless exchanges of the skillsbank.

Individual success stories are not the only benefits skillsbanks confer. Community gains, both general and specific, are part of the reason skillsbanks are emerging all over the country. In economically depressed areas such as Backwoods, a skillsbank can boost every participant's morale; skills swappers are earning livings, improving their lives and living conditions, and physically restoring many parts of the community without the use of money. In Ashland, Oregon, SkillsBank was started in a corner of the Community Food Store five years ago on a very modest scale. Today its offices are in an architectural community showcase in the middle of Lithia Park, a renovated building that had been slated for the wrecking ball by the town since it was a disintegrating eyesore. SkillsBank members put 3,000 hours of work into making over the building and now "lease" it from the city

for a token $1 a year. Comments Gaea Laughingbird of
SkillsBank:

> At the moment, SkillsBank has approximately 450
> members who share among them nearly every
> kind of professional, vocational, and avocational
> background one could imagine. We have horse
> trainers, babysitters, a snake demonstrator, doc-
> tors, plumbers, gourmet cooks, accountants,
> healers, hair stylists, weavers, and electricians.

The people are out there, in your town too, but they
need a way to get in touch with one another.

At the Ashland SkillsBank members' hours are considered equally valuable, and credits and debits are
counted in terms of *hours* which serve as currency.

Hooking Up With a Community Group

The chances are that there is no skillsbank or other
barter organization in your corner of the countryside,
and you don't feel qualified to get one going all by
yourself. Yet you wish there were something like that
around. You'd be a member in a minute. So would
most of us, but somebody has to get the group going.
The most logical beginning for a barter group or
skillsbank is under the wing of an older organization
already well established in the community, such as a
church, any kind of civic organization, a sewing circle,
rod and gun club, the Grange or an old cemetery association. Such groups have already established visibility and credibility, and most of them have buildings,
rooms, or offices easily reachable by most people, an
important point for a barter group. It's easy for any of
these community organizations to hold a trial barter
fair or swap night and test the barter temper of the
community before plunging into formal organization.

There are dozens of helpful information packets, manuals, and books as well as information centers that offer advice on starting up non-profit community exchanges, swap centers, and skillsbanks. Two of the most important sources of help are both programs of VOLUNTEER, The National Center for Citizen Involvement, a nonprofit organization very much involved in counseling and aiding new barter groups. Skillsbank information is available from:

> Bobette Host, Project Coordinator
> VOLUNTEER
> Box 4179
> Boulder, CO 80306

Information on starting a community barter group can be had through

> Dave Tobin
> *Exchange Networks*
> VOLUNTEER
> 1214 16th St., N.W.
> Washington, D.C. 20036

Here are some of the suggestions VOLUNTEER sources offer people interested in getting a neighborhood barter group going. They are all drawn from the experiences of dozens of existing and emerging barter groups all over the country. While most of these have been urban or suburban organizations, the advice has application to rural barter centers.

☞ *Give plenty of time to the planning and design of your barter program*. Plenty of information is available, so use it. The pioneers have gone through most of the problems you're likely to meet, and their *caveats* and suggestions can save your group time and trouble.

☞ *Set up an advisory committee.* Members of this committee should be drawn from the protecting organization or sponsoring group if there is one, from the community residents, clergy, businessmen, community philanthropists, or others who may participate or be affected by the program.

☞ *Start small.* Don't plunge into a grandiose program that risks failure through over-ambition. Work on a small target that means sure success. The example and word of mouth will let your group develop and expand naturally to bigger and better things. "Nothing succeeds like success" was never more true.

☞ *Be sure the group has an office or walk-in center and somebody to run it.* Visibility and availability are of major importance. Nobody wants to get involved in a venture that's a post office box or an extension phone. Part of the first year your barter center will spend much time explaining what it's all about, building up a membership, tracking down and enlisting resources of all kinds. You need a place to do it and a person to do it.

☞ *Seed money is important.* This is the money you need to get started. Of course your group will barter for as much as possible, but not everything can be gotten through trade. Consider that you may need to pay rent for your center (at least a part-time salary to staff), that you will have printing and mailing costs and telephone bills, that you will need office supplies, and that you must pay the inevitable transportation costs for the initial running around putting up posters and notices, giving presentations, and setting up displays to introduce the barter concept and your group to the community.

Where do you get seed money? From the community itself, from grants, from federal, state, foundation, corporate, or church sources, from special fund-raising events, from philanthropists, from universities and community education centers. A helpful source is a training manual on fund-raising for nonprofit citizens' groups by Nancy Mitiguy titled, *The Rich Get Richer and the Poor Write Proposals*.

Getting people in through the door is not always a piece of cake. Experienced skillsbank operators call the early stages of bringing the sheep into the fold "recruitment," and have worked out numerous strategies to show people what a skillsbank is and how it operates, and, finally, to get them involved in the bank. These are some of their tested strategies, to be put into action after you have a good idea of your community's skill needs and the preliminary work.

BARTER COLUMN

In Jupiter Farms, Florida, a small newspaper, *The Country Journal,* which is dedicated to reporting on rural life, has started a good swap column of special interest to country people. Your own local rural newspaper might pick up circulation and perform a community service with a barter column. Here are some samples from *The Country Journal*'s BARTER EXCHANGE.

I would like to barter a pair of white geese for a good working lawn mower and sewing machine. Also one family milking goat for three hour roto-tiller or front-end loader work.

Will trade male beagle, AKC registered, 6 months old, for fencing, building materials or anything of equal value.

Want to trade my pet billy goat and ram for two others, with different blood lines, for breeding.

Free rent of one-bedroom mobile home . . . to mature couple for feeding horse.

Getting the skillsbank application forms to prospective members in a rural area where community interests are bonded and the population relatively sparse is not the headache it can be in large towns and cities or sprawling suburbs. In the country application forms can be left at the general store or passed out after some community function such as Grange meetings, church services, or town meeting. They can also be mailed out, or dropped off at homes by volunteers with cars.

Presentations are another way of getting information and forms to people. At a community gathering a spokesman for the barter group asks for a little time and "presents" a description of what skillsbanks are and can do, and finishes by passing out application forms which can be collected there or mailed in later.

Displays are snappy posters or other eye-catchers accompanying the application forms at places where people tend to gather. In the country, prime spots would be the feed store, a garage, a general store, church bulletin boards, the windows of local banks and businesses, the library, town offices, or a community bulletin board.

Public media pass the word. The radio is still important in rural lives. Many radio stations serving rural populations run a barter program and are pleased to describe and talk about a local skillsbank or swap group. Newspapers and television and radio stations are no strangers to barter. All of them deal in the running problem of blank space or empty air, and because they must use this time and space or lose it forever, they are prime barterers themselves. Sympathetic to barter, they rarely turn down a colorful or human-interest story linked to swapping. Such publicity, however, can tickle a flood of responses. Before you go in for this major publicity, be sure your group is set up to handle it. Experienced workers suggest your skillsbank be fully operational before stories hit the air-waves or the presses.

CHAPTER 5

Barter Clubs

Barter clubs are a modern phenomenon that first saw light in California. Legend has it that the beginnings of the current barter club boom are rooted in North Hollywood, California, where a hardware dealer named Melvin Hilton decided more than three decades ago that he needed his warehouse painted. He told a painter he was willing to swap hardware for the paint job. The painter didn't need any hardware, but his daughter had to have some expensive orthodontic work done. Hilton just happened to know an orthodontist and approached him on the possibilities of a triangular swap—his hardware to the doctor, the orthodontic work to the painter's daughter, and the painter's pigment on Hilton's warehouse. It worked and the Hilton Exchange was off and running, the oldest existent barter club in the country, today worth millions of dollars.

California, with its depression-days barter tradition, its rich soil and perishable fruits of the earth, its affluent and glittery life-styles, swashbuckling real estate entrepreneurs, and diamond-studded tastes for the unusual, is now headquarters for many barter clubs whose chains sprawl all over the country. Imaginative businessmen and *avant garde* horse traders have abandoned the old one-to-one swap and invented the club systems that function like autonomous nations with their own laws, their own currency, and the language of trade. It is estimated that more than 500 barter clubs operate in this country, many of them with affiliated offices and branch outlets, others part of a network of barter franchises.

Barter Clubs

Barter clubs are business organizations. Their members are usually small businessmen, manufacturers, professional people, and craftsmen. They find barter a profitable and useful adjunct to regular cash transactions just as country barter and nonprofit barter organizations ease the harsh difficulties of a pure money economy by trading.

Rural barter is often the economics of necessity, nonprofit barter is self-help in a hostile economic environment, but barter clubs are there to make a profit for somebody. Doctors, real estate dealers, restaurant owners, advertising people, and dozens of others are drawn to barter clubs.

One club, Mutual Credit of Los Angeles, analyzed the first 2,500 transactions of August, 1978, for rough indications of which services and products were most popular. All of the following ranked high and enjoyed vigorous action in the barter club: real estate, restaurants, advertising, dentist, printer, dry cleaner, auto service and repair, hairdresser, jewelry, auto accessories, and landscaping and gardening. In another place and another time quite a different list might emerge, one that reflected the importance of solar-heating products, organically raised food, equipment rental, energy-saving devices, and riding horses.

Barter clubs, like any other business, are profit-making organizations. The entrepreneurs who found barter clubs work hard to attract a membership, recruiting people through word of mouth, friends, advertisements, and salesmen. They use all the latest business techniques—computers, credit cards, "check" books, monthly billing, and newsletters reporting on the safety and desirability of all kinds of investments and collectibles from fine art to diamonds to small town properties.

All of them charge a membership fee, sometimes several hundred dollars, and many also have annual dues. Some charge additional fees for the privilege of trading with members of an affiliated group in another city. Many charge a percentage fee for every between-members swap; some charge both sides of the transaction, others only the "buyer" or only the "seller." Some offer free counseling on barter business techniques to their members, others put out journals and bulletins with articles and business analyses of interest to their trading members. Some preserve their members' anonymity, others do not. All of them put out a bulletin listing the members' needs and haves under various categories. Here are some samples from the Comstock Trading Post's "Marketplace," the publication of this California-based barter club.

Will trade fresh oranges when in season for other edibles in season. Will accept credits or cash between seasons.

DIAMONDS, DIAMONDS, DIAMONDS, DIAMONDS. Gem broker has complete stock of emeralds, rubies, sapphires, and all colored stones. Certified investment parcels, custom jewelry, and large estate jewelry liquidation. Will trade for gold, silver, real estate, money or ???

HAVE: Wormy chestnut cabinet wood ⅜" to 2" thick. Random width and length. Nearly 8,000', 1.25 board ft. unselect. Trade for cash, business van '77–'80, machinery parts or all.

HAVE: MASTIFF puppies. Guard and companion dogs. AKC. Brindle males and females available now. Value $500. Will accept cash, silver, food, tractor, boat, other.

HAVE: Wheelchairs, walkers, hospital beds. Every need for the sick or invalid. Complete equipment and supplies for doctor's offices, clinics, hospitals from otoscopes to complete installations. Will trade for anything we can use. What have you? WE SOLVE PROBLEMS.

Loving care for your pet. Room, board dogs or cats. Will trade for advertising, radio exposure, printing, plumbing, carpentry or ???

Country swappers often find it curious and ironic that barter clubs are so insistent on collecting money payments for dues and transaction fees, but it takes cash to keep the computer wheels turning and the phone bills paid, and nobody starts a barter club out of altruism. Moreover, some clubs will accept part of the fees and dues in member credits, part in cash.

Caveat emptor—let the buyer beware—is a rule in barter club membership, for there are no state or federal regulations—yet—that provide guidelines for barter organizations as there are for banks, the food industry, and professionals. Nor are the barter clubs self-regulated as some professional bodies are. Anyone can start a barter club out of his hat and be free to issue scrip, credits, zingtwiddles, or whatever form of tender he wishes, and free to draw up simple or complicated and tricky rules that force members to play the swapping game his way only.

Each club has a set of rules attached to the membership contract that each new member is obliged to sign, and these can be a bulky bundle of pages. You can expect to find the following general rules in most barter clubs.

"Strange name for a horse. . . ."

1. Members pledge *not* to trade with each other outside the club's system. (To do so would be to avoid the club's transaction fees.)

2. After every trade between members credits must be deposited with the central office within a brief time span, usually a week.

3. Undeposited credits may *not* be passed on to third parties, members or non-members, but must go through the club's central computer and fee-billing machinery.

4. Members must trade with each other if they are able to do so. A member cannot refuse to swap unless he is *on hold,* which means he has accumulated a

specific amount of credits and is "holding" until he can spend some of his piled-up credits.

5. Members are not allowed to jack up the values of their goods or services to gain further trade leverage.

6. Dues and fees must be paid in money or credits when billed or the member's credit account can be frozen and his trading privileges halted until he pays up. Many clubs now collect fees through electronic transfers directly from members' bank accounts, Master Charge or Visa accounts. Others deduct the fee at the central office *before* the exchange goes through.

7. Procedural changes and new rules can be issued by the club at any time. Members must accept the rules or retire from the club.

There are fair and honest traders and club owners, just as there are greedy and unscrupulous people on both sides. Fortunately, the upright and ethical outnumber the shady. Here are some of the evils both members and managers must watch out for.

Members Beware!

Many clubs set limits up to which members *must* accept trade. But some have sky-high limits. Don't let yourself be conned into joining one of these. A common ploy is for a member who has accumulated staggering credits with nowhere to spend them, to rope an unwary person into the organization, then "lay off" his credits on the new member. Indeed, the new member may find himself *bombed out,* or rushed by old members who are heavy-laden with unspendable credits, and who snap up all the new member's goods and leave him with the unspendables. This usually happens just before the final disintegration of a badly run club, and the new member is left holding the bag. No wonder he develops a hatred for swapping.

Another disagreeable con from above is for club owners to float too many of their own credits. Usually they give these extra credits to themselves in order to buy from unwary members. The results are disastrous, for the "currency" is devalued and after a while nobody wants it. Trade languishes or proceeds sluggishly at inflated values for the goods and services swapped. Finally, new members are suckered in and bombed out. A sorry ending.

Some members who amass large numbers of credits find they are offered dubious real estate deals by the management. A California optometrist piled up $14,000 worth of credits in three months, and there was nothing for him to spend this large amount on except real estate. A plumber and his wife gained $500 worth of credits as members of one of the major West Coast clubs, but had trouble spending them. The members they contacted treated them as second-class customers, and either raised prices over their normal level or put the couple off. When they complained to the management, they were offered a piece of property for which there was no access.

Before you join *any* barter club, get from the management a random list of members, and call them up. Find out how they like the organization, whether they have trouble spending credits, how long they've been members. Ask them how they'd like to take some of *your* credits as soon as you join. If they hesitate and hem and haw, find out why.

Headache Members

Barter club owners generally have a liberal dash of wheeler-dealer instincts, and count on their members to have placid and accepting temperaments, people who are satisfied with simple trades and whose greedy itch is scratched by an occasional "deal." Most members are like this, but not all of them. Some are just as aggressive and eager as the club managers, and vigorously use the club for their own ends. These people tend to join several barter clubs at once, to be aggressively alert to bargains, and can haggle and deal with the best of them. Some persuade the management to readjust the rules of the organization by special written-in clauses beneficial to them before they'll join.

A few of these horse traders try to evade the club's fees, and make deals with other members outside the organization while using the club's membership directory for contacts. Some boost the values on their goods and services unmercifully before they start trading. Some who want a particularly desirable commodity (for which they've already arranged a later profitable swap) will offer to pay more in credits than the listed value in order to get the goods. This can start a wildfire of inflation that burns every member before it dies out.

TRADER TYPES

Experienced swappers recognize a dozen types of traders, not only distinct personality types, but people who habitually practice specific barter techniques that link them to a pattern of behavior. Here are a few of these types.

The Honest Trader: Ethical, cooperative, determined that both parties shall benefit from a trade, and whose word, when given, is the Rock of Gibraltar, the Honest Trader keeps the game going. Most traders make a real effort to match this ideal.

The Horse Trader: This fellow is sharp, conniving, well-informed, and a good if opportunistic judge of human character. He's not above doctoring up his goods with paint or razzle-dazzle to pass them off for more than they're worth. He's capable of misrepresenting what he's trading by lies of omission.

The Compulsive Winner: This trader *has* to come out on top of a trade or it's not worth his time. The need to win or triumph over another is what bartering is all about to him. The only way he can trade is up.

The Cheat: This fellow works a con game called "bait and switch." Samples of his goods look great, and the price is right, but when the other trader takes delivery he discovers the goods are of poorer quality than the samples he was shown. A country trader once swapped some livestock for a hundred pairs of rubber chore boots of excellent quality. When he got home with the boxes he discovered they were all—except for the display box—left foot boots.

The Hustler: Always busy, always trading. In a diner he tries to swap for a cup of coffee; at the movie ticket window he keeps on swapping. He talks deals in his sleep and gets crazy thrills out of trading, but it is the number of deals rather than the quality of swaps that drives him on. Most of his swaps are very minor league.

Second-Thought Charlie: After a swap is concluded, this trader starts reconsidering. He's sure he could have gotten more. Soon he feels aggrieved and cheated, and tries to reopen the deal, complaining that he was not treated fairly and demanding a readjustment. After a few of these exhibitions other traders run when they see him coming.

The Bicycle Pump: This trader always inflates the value of his goods before he swaps, usually well above his advertised prices. He claims this is the only way he can show a profit after paying club dues and fees.

Disorganized Dave: This disorganized trader loses notes, forgets deals, is vague about the quality and quantity of his goods, and his bookkeeping is a nightmare of scribbles, loose

pages, missing entries, and mistakes. He is always late for appointments and delivery of goods. Other traders think he is a pain to do business with.

The Dreamer: The dreamer makes wonderful offers pivoting on goods he *thinks* he's going to get, and services he *might* have a call on. He deals in jewels and gold and castles—in talk. In reality he rarely has anything tangible to offer in trade.

The Shrewdie: He knows everything. He reads auction catalogs for relaxation, keeps abreast of collecting trends and news events. He trades very well from a power position of knowledge, experience, reputation, and goods or services up front. He rarely deals in anything but "hard" goods— Krugerrands, quality gems, precious metals, and choice real estate. He's likely to be a barter club owner rather than a member.

Exchange Networks

Exchange networks are the newest wrinkle in profit barter circles. They operate on a more sophisticated and more regimented level than most barter clubs. One of the first exchange networks was the International Trade Exchange, better known as ITE. This business organization has its headquarters in the metropolitan Washington, D.C., area. The organization took the concept of the barter club as its starting point and established a system of linked barter *franchises* all along the East Coast.

ITE has a highly developed marketing program and even sends out account executives to businessmen in various cities to persuade them to buy into the ITE network. In its first year ITE logged more than $2 million in trades, and claims it would have taken a barter club five years to do this. ITE has a trading floor in Washington and trade brokers. Affiliated exchanges match up telephone trade orders from all over through the lightning efficiency of computers. Daily trading sessions top $15,000, even though most of the swaps are small. The success of this and other trade networks is based on their attitude that barter is to be used as an adjunct to regular cash and money-oriented business, and that the attractiveness of "cashless" bargaining lies in its simplicity and speed.

The cost of a franchise license from ITE varies with the kind and size of population in the proposed "target" area, but is reported to average around $20,000. On the local level, the owner-manager of an ITE affiliate screens applicants to be sure the membership has a healthy spread of occupations. Too many plumbers or bakers or doctors in a group can mean some of them will not get much trade business. Members receive credit cards and a catalog listing the other members, their skills, services, and goods. Monthly statements show debits and credits.

In one ITE franchise, members pay $200 to join, plus annual dues of another $100. There is an additional service charge of 10 percent on every transaction between members. Each new member is guaranteed at least $300 worth of business annually or his fee is refunded.

The big barter clubs and exchange network franchises do millions of dollars' worth of trade annually, but the figures do not represent only the sum of members' transactions. Some clubs launch off into the real big time and become involved in swapping warehouses full of goods, million-dollar media barter, and *due bill* swapping, as resort and hotel room credits and restaurant privileges are called.

Giants of the Barter World

Barter clubs and exchange networks are small stuff compared to the barter empires of men who deal in huge trade agreements between corporate giants and

---

HATCH & EDGERTON offers: ". . . Buck, Beaver, Kidd and Russian Fur *Gloves*, . . . sheeting, HARD WARE and CUTLERY, . . . *Splendid Looking Glasses;* Brass fine Setts; Reflectors; Bronzed Lanterns; Brittania and Black Tin Tea and Coffee Pots, &c.

WEST INDIA GOODS and GROCERIES; Nails; Glass; Salt; Fish; Shovels; Cordage; Axes; Furnaces; Linseed and Sperm Oil; Paints; Dye Stuffs; Soap; Indigo; Bottles; Stone Ware, etc. etc.

Most kinds of produce received in exchange for goods.

Vermont Republican & Journal,
Windsor, Vermont, Dec. 10, 1831

nations. These swaps may involve ideologically op-posed countries, very big business, entrepreneurs, and government representatives in reciprocal trades and complex commodity exchange agreements. It is es-timated that 40 percent of all world trade is done through barter, and that in the Western countries, the latest nations to jump on the barter bandwagon, the figure is up to 10 percent and rising. Many Communist and so-called "Third World" countries refuse western currency and insist on exchanging their manufactured goods, raw materials, or agricultural products for western technology, machinery, and equipment. This shift toward barter has increased as currencies have wobbled and tottered and lost their stable footing and reputations. For example, Yugoslavian airlines par-tially paid for planes from the Douglas Aircraft Divi-sion of McDonnell Douglas Corporation with canned meats, power transmission lines, tools, leather goods, and many other products. Union Carbide Corporation swapped the rights and technology to the Russians to build and operate a polyethelene factory. In return they "bought" the factory's production of poly for re-sale in western Europe. In a similar swap, Wilkinson Sword Ltd. put up a razor blade factory for the Rus-sians in return for a percentage of the output. Massey-Ferguson erected a tractor factory in Poland and took a percentage of the Polish tractors produced on the assembly line as barter "payment" for the plant.

In New York the big business bartering firm of At-wood Richards disdains swaps of less value than $500,000 and reports business of more than $100 mil-lion a year. This firm, which began life back in the late Fifties swapping television advertising time for studio equipment and services, now handles anything—*anything*—that can turn a profit. Bat guano, Convair 880s, herbicides, hedge trimmers, pool tables, pizzas, hockey sticks, and computer time are only a few items the firm has traded. Moreton Binn, the owner and president of Atwood Richards, has described the intricacies of a normal deal:

> We traded some imitation mayonnaise to an ocean cruise company for cruise credits which we traded to a printer in exchange for printing credits. We used those credits to print brochures for a digital clock and took a supply of clock radios in exchange and traded them to a hotel chain for room and board credits. We traded those credits to TV stations, which used them for sales meetings, and took advertising time which we gave to the mayonnaise company.

Binn explains the appeal his organization has to manufacturers, importers, and exporters by citing an

———◆◈◆———

Although there are half a dozen legendary barter kings in Europe who live in a shadowy splendor like exiled Renaissance princes, North America has produced its own swap wizards. One is Dr. Armand Hammer, now president of the Occidental Petroleum Co., who went as his father's emissary to Russia in 1921 to collect outstanding bills owed the family pharmaceutical company. He was appalled at the starving population, the dead and half-dead ". . . waiting to be rolled into their trenchlike graves and the pleading faces of thousands of children at the windows of the special train."

Motivated in part by compassion, Hammer offered the Russians a million bushels of wheat that he didn't yet have, in exchange for a million dollars' worth of ancient art, including gem-encrusted icons and Czarist jeweled trinkets, plus caviar, rich furs, leather, and other goods that couldn't directly feed the famine-riddled population. He was 23 years old. This marked the beginning of an astounding lifetime of major barter deals, close relations with the Russians, and work to amass one of the world's great art collections. 🦋

example of a manufacturer of sporting goods who finds himself stuck with $2 million wholesale worth of baseball equipment at the end of the season. The company doesn't want to store the equipment in warehouses until next season.

Instead of "dumping" the goods on the market at a quarter of their value, a common-enough practice, this manufacturer goes to Atwood Richards. He is allowed a credit for the entire $2 million value that he can draw on for any number of things—advertising space and time, cars for salesmen, printing, equipment, office furnishings, hotel and resort accommodations for company meetings, travel fares—all the things the manufacturer will need eventually in the course of business, even bat guano and imitation mayonnaise, should he wish. By swapping, the manufacturer has gotten rid of his warehouse clog, has opened up his inventory, has improved his cash flow situation and conserved his cash outlay, and it all looks better on his books to stockholders. The flexibility of barter is indispensable to the staunchest supporters of the money economy— manufacturers, businessmen, wholesalers, and retailers.

Barter is free from currency regulations and makes international swapping simpler and swifter than the headache of dealing with shifting money values and restrictions on currency exchanges.

International barterers can manipulate different economic systems to their own advantage.

Scarce commodities, limited supplies of raw materials, and vital basic foodstuffs are more often bartered than bought and sold among nations. Uranium, wheat, gold, titanium and other rare metals, soybeans, rice, oil, and a handful of other vital supplies are too important to give up for mere money. Each country must use its most desirable commodities to insure itself a share of the materials and foodstuffs it does not have. Only through barter can this happen.

Computers

The success of barter clubs and franchises, of inter-corporate and international swaps, is not only a reflection of the needs of the times, but is tied to the swift and efficient assembling of data, ranging from estimates on global wheat, soybean, and rice crops to the matching of "haves" and "wants" in a small trade club. Computers have made it possible to handle the tremendous volume of swaps and the variety of skills, goods, services, and information. Comments Bill Austin, the owner and director of the Trade Exchange in Portland, Maine, an ITE affiliate with 300 members and five branch offices:

We couldn't do it without a computer. In 1977 when we started, our total volume was $29,000 worth of exchanges. Last year we were up to $600,000 and this year I think we should go to over $1.5 million.

Business Exchange of Los Angeles, one of the oldest and largest barter clubs, has over 30 offices and more than 5,000 members. The success of BX, as it's known in barter circles, is directly linked to its high-speed computerized accounting system. Founder M. J. McConnell has commented that when he started the club, computerization was in its early days and not a very useful tool. He lost money for nine years. Only when computer technology became sophisticated enough to handle the ebb and flow of a tide of barter offers and counter-offers, the complex transactions, the warp and weft of debit and credit, did the barter club boom take off like a rocket.

Should You Join?

But what do country people have to do with barter barons, humming computers, urban swap clubs, and trading franchises? If you live in the country, should you even consider a barter club? If you are a business person, a craftsman, or a professional, if you make firkins in your garage woodworking shop and have them stacked to the ceiling all over the place, if you have a producing peach orchard, if you have land to trade, if you run a country inn or restaurant, if you operate a ski resort or hunting lodge, if you are a blacksmith, a basket-maker or a wood-carver, if you're a fishing guide or manage a country newspaper, membership in a barter club or exchange organization may be helpful and useful to you; it may even be indispensable. If you have business expertise, a gift for swapping, *and* a local population that can support such an organization, perhaps an exchange franchise or club affiliation will suit you well. Be warned, however, that of all the barter clubs listed, few are in rural areas.

Before you join, remember that barter clubs are strictly business. If you have dealings with the business world, you may be one of those people who can benefit from profit barter organizations, but if you're a country homesteader thinking in terms of cabbage and honey, goat milk and wood-cutting, this kind of barter is probably not for you. Still, barter clubs and exchanges can offer real advantages to some people, even if they live in the country. Craftsmen, professionals, and rural business people join barter clubs because they want and need the contact with a large number of swapping members for many reasons.

☞ You may want to increase your business by contacts with hundreds of new people. Many professionals are restricted from drumming up trade through advertising. For them a barter club is attractive because it announces them and calls them to the attention of its members.

☞ You may be struggling along trying to cope with the strangling coils of inflation and devalued money; your cash flow may be so limited that you can't get your country business off the ground. A barter club with its lure of cashless exchanges will allow you to gain goods and services without money at the same time that it frees your limited cash for vital non-swap expenses.

☞ You may find membership in a barter club attractive because it represents the opening of another channel of credit that translates into more buying power.

☞ You may have to move perishable goods, radio or television advertising time, or magazine or newspaper space that is transitory by nature. Through a barter club you can swap your ripe peaches, air space, and empty columns, which *have* to be used or lost forever, for all sorts of goods and services.

☞ You may see certain tax advantages in swapping goods at wholesale prices, or in even-steven swaps.

☞ You may like the club's computerized bookkeeping services, which free you of many of the headaches and expenses of record-keeping and paperwork.

☞ You may see a way through club membership to "luxury" trading—the chance to get jewelry, a Jacuzzi tub, a new stereo, airline tickets, deluxe accommodations at glamorous resorts, dinners in prestigious restaurants, and other extras without using cash.

☞ The contact with a wide variety of business opportunities through the club's central listings may spark the imaginative and eager trader into new and profitable channels of business.

☞ One of the most compelling reasons members join a barter club is that they feel they are partially escaping from a draconian money system, that they are gaining a little more personal control over their own economic lives and fortunes. Even if no pleasantly fat profits show at the end of a year's bartering, you may like belonging to a club for the satisfaction of working trades instead of clicking around and around as only another gear in the impersonal complexities of the modern capitalist system.

☞ Finally, some people join barter clubs because they think they see an opportunity to slip out from under endless and heavy taxation and government regulation. They should know that the IRS has its eye on barter clubs and escape through barter is usually a dream.

Here are a few country situations that can be improved by membership in a barter club.

Zachary is a potter living in an old farmhouse in upstate New York. He specializes in *avant garde* abstract teapots and foot baths that appeal to other artists, collectors, and museums, but not to the local rural population. Zachary makes a bare living through sales to fine shops and a few select craft outlets, but he wants to swap for "extras." Membership in a barter club gives him this option.

Dr. Zip, the plastic surgeon, gets very restless during March mud-time in his bucolic retreat. He longs for sunny beaches, sparkling blue water, and some exciting sport fishing. Barter club membership lets him trade his skills—or a stay in *his* house—for airline fares and accommodations in the Caribbean.

Billerica also makes pottery in a farmhouse studio, but of a more utilitarian kind than Zachary's. Plates, cups, sugar bowls, platters and saucers, all decorated with her unique wildflower stamp, are packed in boxes by the hundred. But competition is fierce in the handmade pottery business, and Billerica, who is a good potter but a poor businesswoman, doesn't know how to move her inventory. Membership in a barter club and trade, partly for cash, partly for credit, opens up new customer contacts for her, gives her access to some badly needed advertising, keeps her records straight, and provides some cash.

Teddy and Freddy run a country inn with spectacular views and superb food. Because they are new, word-of-mouth has not yet brought them an established clientele; because they are off the beaten track they get no transient trade; because they are financially overextended they can't afford advertising. Barter club membership draws the attention of the membership to them and allows them to trade rooms and meals for advertising, new furnishings, winter snow removal services, air-shipped lobsters every Thursday, landscaping of an unusual formal garden, a re-upholstering job on the fireside sofas, and a van to pick up vacationers at the airport forty miles away.

Philomena runs a ski shop near a famous ski center during the winter; in the summer she carries a line of camping and mountain climbing equipment. Last year, despite statistical predictions and hope, almost no snow fell. Philomena sold virtually no skis and was threatened with financial disaster in the spring. Not only was her shop still crammed full of ski equipment,

---

HAVE 4 acres in Ramona, CA. Water, utilities, 2 miles to town. Value: $49,500. WANT: Single family residence anywhere in Sun Belt, construction equipment, single engine aircraft, or hot tubs.

Comstock Trading Post, February, 1980

leaving no room for the summer camping and climbing gear, but she had no money to stock up on her summer line. Membership in a barter club allowed her to swap her entire ski inventory for credit at retail prices, and, for a small cash fee, to spend her credits on the needed hiking and camping goods at wholesale, plus gain the attention of 5,000 traders. For her, club membership became future insurance that, despite the quixotic vagaries of Mother Nature, her investment was protected. Somewhere there would always be snow, and a trader willing to take skis in swap.

UNWRITTEN RULES FOR BETTER BARTER

There are rules and guides to smooth business trading dictated by tradition, and an unwritten code of ethical behavior. Barter is largely conducted verbally in an informal way, and new swappers and club members are carefully watched by the old hands to see how they conduct themselves. Here are some general attitudes and traditional rules that experienced and good barterers follow.

ᛆᛉ A trader's word is his or her bond. Once you have given your word and have shaken hands on a deal it *must* be honored. If you renege on a deal, the word will get around fast, and in short order you'll find yourself ostracized by other traders.

ᛆᛉ Competitiveness, the will to win, victory over an opponent, cornering the market, supremacy—all these aggressive attitudes can be hindrances to good bartering. In an exchange *both* parties must be satisfied with the deal; if there is a "winner" there must also be a "loser" and a losing trader will rapidly lose interest in barter.

ᛆᛉ In disputes and problems, cooperative bargaining should guide both traders. Above all else, a good trader is as flexible as an eel. Rigid, unyielding, aggressive personalities make poor traders.

CHAPTER 6

Real Estate

Land is the bedrock basis of all country living. It has been valued at all times in history and at all places on earth where people live because it is finite and because human beings can scratch a living from it. It has become extraordinarily valuable in recent decades. An exploding world population has led to nightmarish predictions of human beings jamming every available bit of land, living mean and sorry lives.

The current housing shortage and terrific cost of construction have made the individual vacation home both desirable and difficult to achieve. The remorseless increase in food costs, which seems to parallel a decrease in quality, has awakened a new interest in gardening and fruit tree growing on at least a few acres. A rising fear of city life with its climbing crime rate and increasingly wretched schools tips the balance toward the nostalgic lure of small town and rural stability and neighborliness. The back-to-the-land movement has spread in the past two decades from left-wing hippie homesteaders to right-wing investment counselors. Land and real estate, both for homes and investment purposes, are considered by many to be the most desirable kind of material possession on earth, superior to stocks and bonds, to gold and diamonds. Unencumbered land and real estate, free and clear of mortgages or liens, is valuable, and rural land, especially good farmland, has value in terms of life support, survival, and production far beyond its market dollar value. Land parcels are major counters in big-league barter.

Andrew Carnegie, who knew something about wealth, said once that 90 percent of all millionaires had heaped up their piles through real estate investment, and went on to advise that "More money has been made in real estate than in all industrial investments combined. The wise young man or wage earner should invest his money in real estate."

That advice is still sound and still followed by the readers of investment journals and newsletters. Trading land and real estate has been a traditional and fairly secure route to wealth since ancient times. Ultimately land is the basis of almost all wealth—cropland, grazing land, minerals and ores, timber, fossil fuels, communication and trade routes, residential sites, and market towns. Real estate dealers are fond of pointing out that famous early swap that still makes the school books, the 1649 barter between the Dutch and the Indians of Manhattan of a few axes, some bread, a gun, six strings of wampum, some knives, bells and beads for a piece of land that has become one of the major marketplaces on earth. The owner of a barter franchise likes to hand out copies of this deal to new members just to illustrate the power of barter.

Rural swapping yarns celebrate clever traders who swapped peach trees for plantations, cows for good farms, or jackknives for granite quarries as one determined New Hampshire fellow did in the last century. Some shortsighted rural landowners have traded so-called "worn out" farmland to the gravel excavators and topsoil sellers in return for a share of the fat profits. Other farmers who have watched nearby urban centers expand steadily over the years have ended by swapping the back and the front forty for a piece of the action in a new shopping mall or housing development or industry sited where lately his cows had roamed.

Present-day swaps range from home exchanges by two parties who each yearn for a change of scene to corporate trades by men who see fast-food joints at the end of every corn row and the silver of dimes and quarters in the waters of every lake.

Not all land and real estate swaps are success stories. There are dozens of examples of speculative trading in real estate that ended in rock-bottom smashes with fortunes lost and lives ruined. In the Florida boom of the 1920s hundreds of small investors lost their shirts when the rhetoric-tinged dreams of palm trees and sunshine turned into nightmares of hurricane-lashed swampland and waterlogged lots. Again, in 1974, the Florida condominium rush faded away and left many tail-end speculators holding empty bags.

Thousands of men and women make a living out of real estate and land investment, either through teaching and telling others (for a price) how to make money swapping up and pyramiding holdings, or through active trade in land and real estate.

A tried-and-true technique in land swapping is to acquire cheaply or on margin, land that you suspect or know is going to appreciate in the short run through highway construction, shopping mall erection, the expansion of an exclusive residential area, the coming exploitation of water or mineral or fuel rights or other wealth-producing projects. Land-swapper entrepreneurs sometimes make shrewd guesses about these probable developments, sometimes have inside information, sometimes engineer and maneuver the desired expansion or exploitation in the direction they want, or—very rarely—are lucky enough to hit the land appreciation jackpot through chance.

Cowboy Jack was the son and heir of a longtime Texas farm family. The family acres started out twenty-five miles away from Dallas a few generations back. By the time Cowboy Jack's parents died, leaving him the farm, the city was in the backyard and moving fast. Cowboy Jack bartered a share of his proposed development to an interested contractor, slapped in a big shopping mall, leased the space on very attractive terms to dozens of shops and businesses, parleyed his shopping mall credits into ultra-deluxe housing on the rest of the farm, and in no time had piled up his first million.

Land and real estate barter deals are often stories of one person's gain in personal wealth by trading productive farmland for industrial, developmental, and residential use. The loss of rural farmland solely to line the pockets of developers and fast-buck real estate operators is becoming a national crime in this country. Slowly, individual states and even towns are beginning to guard against this trend, by introducing legislation and town planning that protects farmland from exploitation and development. Many planners believe that the future holds widespread food shortages and astronomical food prices that will hit hardest the regions that import the most food. Independence and self-sufficiency through local food production is seen as an answer to the food supply problem. In this scenario farmland becomes critically important. Cabbages and carrots, soybeans and sorghum don't grow well in macadam and concrete.

Shady Stuff

Some people deal in real estate and land exchanges in a way that treats the land not as something precious and fecund, but as a kind of commodity with a value. To them a piece of land is immovable currency. The most desirable properties to these traders are the income properties like apartment houses, condominiums, shopping centers, developments, agri-biz

farms, choice waterfront resort property and, in the "survival-disaster-market," remote, sheltered properties with underground quarters and subterranean water supplies. All of these are swapped shrewdly and are major barter transactions often carried on by professional real estate traders. The small stuff of this world—tiny irregular pieces of land situated in slums and run-down urban areas, landlocked properties without access, land contaminated by chemicals or hazardous wast disposal, land abutting an air-fouling factory, or a strip mine, or an oil tank storage area, swampland, desert, floodplains, and the rarefied atmosphere of mountain tops along with a hundred other conditions that render the property nearly valueless through the hands of man or nature—is often swapped by sharpie traders to innocents looking for "a real estate investment." To too many people land is land, and they assume there is something magical about it simply because it *is* land.

Almost always the sharpie trader passes on his dismal parcels without ever having seen them himself, and for a very good reason; once the bad features are seen and known, the trader is under an obligation to describe the property realistically in any future trade. For example, suppose you as a novice barterer have accumulated a few thousand dollars' worth of goods or services or credits. It's natural to think almost immediately of "investing" in a piece of land. A fast-talking trader can convince you to take his particular bit of the planet. But when you go to take a proud and proprietory look at your investment, you discover it is a boggy sinkhole on the outskirts of Newark where old crankcase oil and bedsprings have been dumped since 1935. Even worse than the sting of recognition that you have been had, is the bitter realization that now that you have seen it, you must, in all fairness, tell anyone *you* trade with about its drawbacks. If you go a-complaining to the sharpie who shoved the thing onto you, he can claim righteously, "Gee, I never looked at the property—had no idea there was anything wrong. Too bad, fella, but I didn't know. Well, you win some, you lose some!"

AVOID GETTING BURNED IN REAL ESTATE SWAPS

If you are swapping for land outside your community with an unknown trader, proceed as though you were paying gold earned by hard labor in the salt mines.

• Look at the piece of land or property in question *before* swapping.

• Get a lawyer, a title search, a warranty deed, and a title guarantee as well as full information of any and all encumbrances.

• Get all the conditions and facets of the swap in writing.

Passing a known bad deal on to some other unsuspecting trader is called "the bigger fool" principle in action, and is highly unethical.

Real Estate Investment Barter

Reputable real estate and land swappers like cashless transfers of investment land and property for one major reason: there is no capital gains tax on these swaps as there is on sales. Charles Morrow Wilson called the federal capital gains tax "one of the most devastating destroyers of private ownership of wealth. . . . " and land buyers and sellers still agree with him. Through barter, capital gains taxes can be deferred for many years or even the trader's lifetime by judicious swapping, under a tax code section known to traders as the parent of "1031 exchange." In no way does a 1031 exchange permanently avoid the payment of capital gains taxes. It merely postpones the day until the trader decides to cash in his property holdings, and at that point he has to pay up the tax that year on his gain.

Many trader-investors follow a simple but effective strategy: they seek out property that is undervalued, not because of any irremediable or inherent flaw in the land or building, but because of poor appearance, rundown and neglected condition, bad management of the property, or other reversible problem. The imaginative and astute investor, who has recognized the potential possibilities long before the actual swap, then smartens up his new property my making needed repairs, installing up-to-date equipment, drawing in more and wealthier customers or tenants through advertising or other means, and in every way increasing the income-making potential of the investment. All of this results in a *higher valuation* on the property. Now the trader barters off his improved property for another piece or pieces of real estate in kind and of matching value. He continues trading up, always on apparent even-steven exchanges. Over a period of time he will have worked up to a very much more valuable property than he started with, all without paying a dollar of capital gains taxes. Inflation will have pushed the paper value of his most recent holdings even higher.

Real estate investors tend to regard raw land as non-income-producing property, and generally shy away from it. However, country people know there's a staggering difference between the raw land 2,000 feet up the side of a rocky mountain and the land lying level and smooth along the fertile river valley. There's also a big difference between the productive, well-drained, and enriched land of a properly managed farm and the brush-clogged, eroded brier patches of an old place that's lain unworked for generations. Poor farmland can be bought or traded for at low values, then improved by clearing, ditching, draining, manuring, liming, and growing green cover crops. Over a period of time the value of this raw land will increase well beyond the current market value, because it will have become productive.

If the land has a salable commodity on it like pulp wood or firewood (both renewable resources), or a sugar bush for maple syrup production, or an old orchard that needs pruning and rejuvenation to get it back into paying production, *make the land pay for itself*. If there are hayfields, swap or sell the hay, manure the fields, and increase the yield. Hay is expensive these days. Land that simply lies dormant, that sucks cash from your pocket in taxes and upkeep without producing some income or consumable produce, is a liability. Unless you have the ability or the imagination to *make* your land productive, you do not have a real estate investment—you have a speculation.

You are speculating that the land will increase in value over time all by itself. You gamble that the increase will be greater than that of the inflation rate, gamble also that the speculative bubble won't pop and leave you with devalued, non-productive land.

"Like Property"

Under Section 1031 of the Internal Revenue Code, if a property is held for productive use in business or trade, or for investment, and if it is traded for *like property,* no gain or loss on the exchange is recognized, and, as we have seen, no capital gains tax need be paid.

But what is "like property"? This term refers to utility rather than the type of property itself. Investment properties must be traded for investment properties; residences must be traded for residences. You may not swap an income-producing grain elevator for a chalet you expect to live in, nor your bungalow for a bowling alley. You may not trade either your residence or your investment property for stock-in-trade inventory, bonds, notes, diamonds, stocks, and so forth under a "like-for-like" definition. Yet within these lines there is considerable room for maneuvering to suit most traders. An income-producing mushroom farm valued at $60,000 and a small-town laundromat valued at $90,000 with a $30,000 mortgage are considered like properties; a truck farm and a trout hatchery are like properties; a parking lot and a marina, or an apartment house and a shooting preserve are like-for-like in terms of investment possibilities and income production, even though they differ radically in function, appearance, location, and ambiance.

Speculation Fever—Rocketing House Values

In the Seventies house prices went up rapidly and spectacularly, outleaping the price rises of stocks and springing ahead of the awesome inflation rate as measured by the Consumer Price Index. This was not just a regional boom, but a nationwide phenomenon, especially marked in the peripheral rings of settlement around major cities.

Many investment experts expect that this boom, like the Florida real estate bubble and the stock market's blinding rise and crash in 1929, is doomed to bust in the near future. They fear the current housing market is built on the shaky foundations of overextended credit, speculation, and inflation.

People who have owned a house for a few years have been gratified to see its paper value leap dramatically upward, and many have borrowed against the increased market value of their homes. After the borrowed money is gone, if a housing depression occurs, these homeowners will find their houses severely devalued at the same time they are legally saddled with heavy mortgage payments.

For example: Harry and Harpie paid $35,000 for a comfortable house near the shore in 1965. After fifteen years they still owe $12,000 on the mortgage. However, now their house has appreciated remarkably and has a market value of $90,000. Flushed with the thrill of this easily gained wealth, they put another mortgage on the house to the tune of $40,000 and live in style in their $90,000 house. With beef and lettuce prices what they are, the money soon disappears. Comes the crash and the market value of Harry and Harpie's house plummets to $30,000. Harry and Harpie are ruined, for they owe $52,000 on a $30,000 house. Worst of all, they aren't alone, and thousands of homeowners like them default on swollen mortgages.

The "smart money" people who envision this depressing series of events are cashing in their own high-value urban and suburban homes while prices are way up in the air, and they are heading—guess where? Right. They are reinvesting in rural properties of all kinds, working farms, vacation cottages, old houses, and raw land. So desirable have crumbling old farmhouses with sagging roofs and buckled floors become that a monthly newsletter, *The Old-House Journal,* and half a dozen books on restoring, renovating, and repairing these aging buildings are doing well in a faltering publishing market. These people are buying with cash, with credit, or swapping for rural property. Some are retiring to their new estates; some are using the land as a valuable commodity in a restless gallop of trading up toward personal fortunes; some are manipulating working farms for the substantial tax breaks they offer, either on their own or in partnership with other land investors; some have changed their way of life and are homesteading or farming. The most secure new landowners are those who have bartered for their property and own it clear. The most dangerously situated are those who have got their new places through bank loans and financing, and then, after a year or two, mortgaged them further against speculative housing market prices.

Looking for a Home

Not everyone who desires land is a calculating investor. Many people dream of having a few acres of their own in the country as a homestead residence, and if they want to conserve their cash for improving the land and outbuildings, barter or part-barter, part-cash, is a sensible approach.

It is possible to swap labor, services, and goods outright for land. In one small farm community a farmer's widow is happy to swap twenty acres of unused pasture for several prize milk cows. In another community a farmer unable to get steady farmhands swaps a few acres to a young homesteading couple in return for their part-time labor over a period of years. They get a deed and he gets a written agreement.

The absentee owner of a rural woodlot swaps sixty acres to three couples for their labor in selectively logging the property. He gets what he wants—the pulp and cordwood for cash sales, and they get what they want—cleared land for home building.

Another couple short on money but long on imagination and with good experience in restaurant work, approach the owner of an old brick mansion that has fine lines but is in poor repair. They explain their plan to convert the old house into an inn, and suggest a deal: they get a deed to the property and the owner will get a percentage of the inn profits. They are able to show the owner cost figures, projected operating overhead, sample menus, the predicted clientele estimated by a local market analysis outfit; they walk through the old house enthusiastically describing renovations and repairs, much of which they plan to do themselves. The owner is convinced that they have ambition and experience and have planned carefully. He takes the risk. A year later the couple is doing a satisfactory business in their attractive old inn, the former owner is relieved of taxes and upkeep and receives an increasing amount of annual income, while local lovers of good food and drink have a starred item on their lists.

Retired and older people on farms and large land holdings are often willing to swap some of their property for upkeep on the rest; on farmland this could mean cutting brush, fertilizing fields, keeping a woodlot thinned and healthy, haying, checking and correcting erosion problems, mending stone walls, repairing farm roads, and doing the many other chores that *must* be done to keep the land's value as a farm. Neglected farmland means not only loss of current market value, but the loss of generations of back-breaking human labor.

People swap land for goods, too. *Yankee* magazine often runs property barter ads in its roomy "Swoppers' Column." Many barter organizations and clubs also list real estate barters. Here are some examples:

> One-acre building lot in planned community— Lake Arrowhead, Maine. Will swop for 1972–74 Mercedes 280 or equivalent value lot on Cape Cod.

> Wanted: 1953 Cadillac Eldorado convertible, whole car for developed N.Y. lot or Conn. lake lot.

> 5+ acres on . . . Lake, AR. Value: $12,500. Will trade for gold, silver, diamonds, farm equipment, construction equipment, single engine airplane, single-family home anywhere . . .

> 160 acres, Cooperstown, NY—surveyed, scenic country, property, buildings, excellent road frontage, water, utilities, timber and tillable. Value: $65,000. Will trade for coins or collectibles.

If you own land or a house but wish it were somewhere else, selling and then buying in your dream location can be a lengthy, frustrating, and expensive process. Try swapping like-for-like residential property or raw acreage with somebody else.

> Will swop 1¼-acre lot in Lake Mead, Arizona (80 miles from Las Vegas), for lot in Vermont, Maine, or New Hampshire.

Have wooded building lot, all utilities, on green-belt. Clubhouse and golf course, south of Ocala, Florida. Swop for 1–5 acres Maine or New Hampshire.

Members of barter clubs can often use the organization's scrip or credits for a down payment on a piece of property owned by the organization or another member. Antique and luxury automobiles, as well as gold, silver, diamonds, mobile homes, stamps, boats, rare coins, and works of art are frequently bartered for real estate. Whatever you have of value can be traded for land, but almost always the deals will include part cash unless you are swapping properties even-steven.

CHAPTER 7

Barter Taxes

Many people are under the pleasant but erroneous impression that if you barter you need not pay taxes. For most barters, this is simply not true.

Private Exchange of Goods

While Internal Revenue Service agents will concede there is little enforcement and less reporting at the lower level of barter—my tomatoes for your zucchini—they emphatically will not concede that such a barter is not taxable. To do so would place the IRS in the position of drawing a line. If I can barter one tomato, can I barter twelve without paying a tax? A bushel? A truckload? A trainload? Thus they stick to their standards and advise that if I know the cost of my dozen tomatoes—twenty cents, let's say—and I get $1 worth of your zucchini for them, I should report a taxable income of eighty cents.

There is one opportunity for legally avoiding such a tax, and that's on the exchange of used goods. I have a fancy ten-speed bicycle that cost $169. My interests have turned from cycling to photography. You offer to sell your 105mm lens for $100, but will trade it for my bicycle. We trade. I owe no federal income tax on the deal, since I'm in effect selling my bicycle for $100, and so have a loss, not a profit.

This is the reason the IRS shows little interest in garage sales, unless they turn into year-round places of business. A once-a-year sale represents the owner's attempt to get rid of excess and unneeded possessions, and at a loss.

Income

When barter is a demonstratable part of someone's income, the IRS shows greater interest. For example, Dr. Zip, the plastic surgeon, accepted six cords of firewood from Woodcutter Joe for a repair job on Joe's broken nose. Dr. Zip did not report this on his tax returns. He had also accepted a side of bacon, a down comforter, a Western saddle, and an Irish setter pup in trade for his surgical skills, and neglected to report any of these exchanges in his income tax return.

Unfortunately for Dr. Zip, the tax examiner decided to ask him a few questions. The very first one was, "Have you engaged in any bartering in the past year?"

"I cannot tell a lie," replied Dr. Zip reluctantly, and he described his trades. The IRS swiftly ruled that these swaps for his professional services counted as reportable income, and that Dr. Zip owed taxes on several thousand dollars' worth of undeclared income.

In recent years the IRS has become very alert to the huge wave of bartering that is sweeping the country. A recent IRS study indicates that in one year a whopping $75 billion of legally earned income was simply not reported, with a tax loss estimated at $13 to $17 billion. Barter was the most frequently named villain. Not only has the IRS started asking questions about the barter activities of individual taxpayers, but it has started investigating barter clubs and exchanges by the hundreds. While most barter clubs simply leave the reporting of transactions to their members' consciences, some of them keep records of transactions for a year. Some keep no records at all, and some even cater to their members' desire for secrecy by not publishing a membership directory. They will probably not get away with this. The U.S. District Court of Maryland has ruled that a commercial barter club is compelled to identify members in response to an IRS summons.

Many clubs warn their members with the IRS statement that "gross income includes all the income you receive—in the form of money, property, or services—that is not, by law, expressly exempt from tax. . . . Income in any form other than cash is reported at the fair market value of goods or services received."

A recent edition of *The Audit Technique Handbook for Internal Revenue Agents* puts emphasis on the new search for barter practices. Here is what this IRS publication says:

INCOME FROM BARTERING

(1) When verifying income, the examiner should be alert to the possibility of "bartering" or "swapping" techniques or schemes. Such noncash exchanges may be done directly; however, the greater volume of these exchanges is handled through reciprocal trade agencies. Both services and inventory may be exchanged for "credits." These "credits" can then be used to obtain other goods or services. Bartering does result in taxable income and should be reported as such.

(2) Some areas of possible tax abuse are as follows:

(a) Nonrecognition of current income.

(b) The trading of services or inventory for capital assets (which would convert ordinary income to capital gain) or for fixed assets (which should be depreciated over the useful life of the asset).

(c) The exchange of inventory or services for personal goods and services, such as vacations, houseboats, luxury cars, use of vacation home or condominium, or payment of personal or stockholder debts.

(3) During the initial interview, examiners should inquire as to whether the taxpayer was involved in any bartering during that year.

(4) In addition, examiners should be alert for the following:

(a) Deductions and/or payments for credit liability insurance or insurance guaranteeing lines of credit.

(b) Deductions and/or payments for membership fees, annual dues, or service charges or specialized reciprocal trading companies.

(c) The write-off or mark-down of inventory

especially for excess or supposedly obsolete inventory.

(d) The factoring or sale of Accounts or Notes
Receivable to specialized reciprocal trading firms.

It's fairly clear that the IRS maintains that these
exchanges of goods or services constitute income to
both parties and must be reported. In January 1979 the
IRS issued a ruling on the matter (R.R. 79-24) and
outlined two barter situations to illustrate the ruling.

In the first example, a lawyer did some personal
legal services for a house painter who, in return,
painted a house for the lawyer. The lawyer and the
painter, said the IRS, must report as income the fair
market value of the services each received in reporting
gross income.

"How are we supposed to run tanks on broccoli?"

The second case involved a landlord who allowed a professional artist six months of free rent in return for a work of art by the artist. The IRS ruled that the artist and landlord had to include the fair market value of the "income" in their gross incomes.

Barter club credits are very disturbing to the IRS. After a period of confusion, the IRS ruled in January 1980 that for tax purposes the value of each "trade unit" was one dollar.

Yet despite the rulings and the sharp governmental eye on barter there are gray areas where taxpayers can haggle and argue with the tax man. "Fair market value" is one of these areas. Your IRS tax guide says: "Fair market value is defined as the price at which the property would change hands between a willing buyer and a willing seller, neither being under any compulsion to buy or sell, and both having reasonable knowledge of the relevant facts."

Another gray area is the question of mutual gifts, which are tax free as long as neither person was expecting any compensation for his or her "gift." One analyst, looking at the lawyer-painter swap that the IRS offered as an example of taxable income trading, commented:

> What if the lawyer and painter were friends? How could the IRS prove that their services were not mutual gifts, which are exempt from tax?

———◆◆◆———

"I would never ask if these transactions are reported to the IRS and I don't want to know. It's not our role to advise people on the tax treatment of these transactions."

James Matison, president of Pfeister Barter, Inc., a New York trade exchange, as quoted in the *New York Times*, March 15, 1981

Moreover, who is to decide the "fair market value" of the services rendered?

Obviously, under our "voluntary" tax system, the lawyer and painter are expected to estimate themselves how much the income should be. Normally, let's say that the lawyer charges $50 an hour. Is that fair market value? Not necessarily. He may charge more for certain clients, depending on the technical nature of the case, or less for widows and friends. Perhaps he offers discounts from time to time. On other occasions, he donates his time and services to charity.[1]

Tax-Deferred Barter

Some kinds of barter, in addition to exchanges of personal property, are not immediately taxable. The favorite of real estate swappers is Section 1031 of the Internal Revenue Code. It permits traders to exchange "like kind" investment or business properties without paying a capital gains tax until the property is sold for cash or exchanged for something "unlike" it. (See Chapter 6 for a discussion of how traders use this type of exchange.) Here is what the code says:

COMMON NONTAXABLE EXCHANGES, SECTION 1031:

Exchange of Property Held for Productive Use or Investment

(a) Nonrecognition of Gain or Loss from Exchanges Solely in Kind.

---

1. Mark Skousen, "The Tax Advantages of Barter," *How to Barter*, ed. Dave London, Walnut Creek, CA: 1980, p. 16.

No gain or loss shall be recognized if property held for productive use in trade or business or for investment is exchanged solely for property of a like kind to be held either for productive use in trade or business or investment.

Wages in Barter? Watch Out

Just as Dr. Zip was forced to include in his gross income the fair market value of the cordwood and other goods he accepted in return for his professional services, people who receive barter credits or goods and services as part of their wages are supposed to report them. The IRS Bulletin 80-8, February, 1980, outlines a situation.

C is an employee of the barter club. During the taxable year, C, who uses the cash receipts and disbursements method of accounting, received from the club in exchange for C's services gross wages of $20,000, $10,000 in cash and 10,000 credit units. C is entitled to use the credit units in the same manner as other members of the club. However, the club does not charge C a commission on C's barter purchases.

The IRS held that "C must include $20,000 in C's gross income for the taxable year."

The IRS is studying traditional "benefits" not often recognized as barter, such as allowing the children of faculty members free tuition at many colleges and universities. Should a professor have several children attending the college, this could represent a substantial amount. Employee discounts may also be considered as income that should be reported.

An exception is that if the benefit or the goods or services traded to the employee as part of wages are

primarily for the convenience of the employer, they
need not be reported as part of the employee's income.

For example, Prentiss is a fire insurance inspector
who must travel hundreds of miles each week checking businesses. His company provides him with a car.
Although he uses the car for his personal needs as well
as on the job, the car is crucial to the fulfillment of his
job, for without it he couldn't do his inspecting. Prentiss has this car for the good of the hiring company,
and therefore need not report it as part of his income.

Trixie takes a summer job at a girls' camp. The
wages are low, but included are free room and board,
non-taxable because it is essential to her employer that
Trixie be on the premises twenty-four hours a day.

Farmer Plug has a hired man. He provides him not
only with a salary, but with a rent-free tenant house
and the use of a truck. The hired man need not report
these benefits on his income tax return for his presence
in the tenant house and his use of the truck are primarily for the convenience of Plug.

A Barter Hero

In his *Civil Disobedience,* written on the continuing
occasion of his refusal to pay a poll tax, Thoreau ob-
served, "But, if I deny the authority of the State when
it presents its tax-bill it will soon take and waste all my
property, and so harass me and my children without
end. This is hard."

There is a man who has had more than a decade's
experience with the state's harassment over his refusal
to pay taxes. The recently issued second edition of
Charles Morrow Wilson's *Let's Try Barter,* which had
been out of print for some years, has a foreword by
Karl Hess, the closest thing to a barter hero we have.

A decade ago, in his early middle age, Hess was ". . . a very well-salaried, conservative political researcher, an upper-middle-class income earner from the Cadillac, country-club and whiskey-by-the-case set" person. But after fights with the IRS over taxes that Hess refused to pay on moral grounds, culminating in the seizure of his paycheck by two tax collectors at his place of business, Hess revolted. He retired from the money economy and became a "tax resister" after sending the IRS notice of his intentions and a copy of the Declaration of Independence.

Hess took up barter as a way of life, eschewing money and paying no taxes. Royalties from a book Hess wrote were dedicated in advance to charity; the IRS seized them. Yet Hess commented, with gratitude to the IRS, that this confrontation has led him into ". . . the most productive and happy part of my life."[2] Hess acquired and polished barterable skills—welding and metalwork, auto repair, article- and book-writing, lecturing, and much more. For more than ten years he has bartered for nearly everything—the use of a truck, vegetables, building materials, legal services. He owns almost nothing, but enjoys a comfortable life in a house of his own design, swapping through life with enthusiasm and vigor.

Legal Aspects of Barter

Barter agreements are legal contracts. Once you and your swapping partner have agreed on a trade, it's binding in court.

Generally, barter transactions fall under the Uniform Commercial Code which most states have

---

2. Karl Hess, "My Life in Barter," *Oui*, 1977.

enacted. Under the code (UCC 2-201) when goods are exchanged between traders, if the value of the goods is under $500, an oral contract is sufficient to bind, unless there is some inequity or weakness in it, and it will stand up in court. Many traders do business on the proverbial handshake and their given word, even in large transactions. Naturally, these quick, simple, and mutually trusting deals are usually between traders who know each other well and respect each other's word. Almost all country barter is done this way, but many newcomers to swapping are not aware that their casual agreements to swap are binding legal contracts. True, your neighbor is not going to haul you into court because you failed to supply him with half the rabbits from the doe he gave you, but he could.

When goods with a value of over $500 are exchanged, the code says a simple verbal agreement is not enough. There must be some written indication of the swap with the signatures of both traders affixed, or the agreement is not "enforceable." It is an excellent general policy to put swaps into writing if you are dealing with an unknown person for the first time, if you are involved in interstate swapping (different state laws may apply to the trade, and the traders have a choice of which state's laws they follow), if you are trading through the mails, or if the goods and services being exchanged are especially valuable, important, perishable, or in any other way fraught with possible problems and mishaps.

Get Professional Help

Before you get involved in investment or profit barter, before you barter for part of your income, before you join a barter club, find yourself a tax advisor, preferably one who barters. He or she can help you through the treacherous currents of tax and barter rulings, and keep you abreast of legal decisions affecting barter situations.

The line between tax avoidance and tax evasion is sometimes a fine one, but deliberate misrepresentation of your records to avoid reporting bartered goods or services as part of your taxable income is fraud. There is nothing wrong, though, with making every effort to keep your taxes as close to rock bottom as possible.

Anyone may so arrange his affairs that his taxes shall be as low as possible; he is not bound to choose that pattern which will best pay the Treasury; there is not even a patriotic duty to increase one's taxes.

Judge Learned Hand

INFORMATION SOURCES

Here are books, publications, and sources of information on how to barter, how to start a barter group, how to make contact with real estate swappers, how to improve country real estate, as well as a concise listing of barter organizations and clubs.

Nonprofit Barter Group Information

If you are interested in starting a nonprofit barter group or skillsbank in your community, many of the existing groups that have struggled through the early difficulties and emerged victorious can help you. They have made up packets of valuable information based on their experiences, to help you get your barter group off on the right foot.

Useful Services Exchange of California
Director: David Downing
USE of California
7443 Aldea Avenue
Van Nuys, CA 91406

For $2.50 you receive a packet of information on USE with sample forms, a brochure, and a copy of the newsletter.

Community Skills Exchange
921 North Rogers Street
Olympia, WA 98502

For $2 they will send you a packet including their own
history, current office procedures, and the problems
they encountered and solved.

R. Kay Fletcher and Stephen B. Fawcett. *The Skills
Exchange.* 55 pp., 1979, $6. This is a practical manual
for beginning barter organizers. It contains full details
on record-keeping and providing information and outreach to the community. It lists the responsibilities of
the exchange, and evaluates the program. Write to:

> The Center for Public Affairs
> University of Kansas
> Lawrence, KA 66045

Barter Network
930 Temalpais Avenue
San Rafael, CA 94901

For $5 the Barter Network will send you a packet of
information on their program, copies of brochures,
skills listings, an interviewer's guide, and more.

Sharing Work and Products (SWAP). SWAP offers an
excellent information packet which includes a complete copy of A. Lloyd and P. Segal's *The Barter Research Project,* a summary of the First National Barter
Conference, and material on SWAP's own program.
$10. Write:

> SWAP
> 29 South Mills
> Madison, WI 53715

Give and Take
135 Church Street
Burlington, VT 05401

For $5 Give and Take will send you a packet of information on their history, problems, and solutions.

A number of books, newsletters and manuals are in circulation with up-to-date advice on fund-raising and nonprofit exchanges.

Seymour B. Sarason and Elizabeth Lorentz. *The Challenge of the Resource Exchange Network*. Jossey-Bass, 1979. $13.95.

Exchange Networks, ed. Dave Tobin. An extremely useful bimonthly newsletter linking all sorts of nationwide nonprofit barter groups. Write:

> *Exchange Networks*
> VOLUNTEER
> 1214 16th St., N.W.
> Washington, DC 20036

Nancy Mitiguy. *The Rich Get Richer and the Poor Write Proposals*. Amherst, MA. $5 plus $.50 postage. A training manual on fund-raising for nonprofit citizen groups with information on how to find funding sources, whether federal, foundation, corporate or church; how to get the community involved in the project; grassroots fundraising; proposal writing and much more. Write:

> Citizen Involvement Training Project
> 138 Hasbrouck
> University of Massachusetts
> Amherst, MA 01003

Putnam Barber, Richard Lynch, and Robin Webber. *MiniMax: The Exchange Game*. 1979. $21.95. This is a multipurpose training "game" with playing cards, and flip chart sheets that lead the players to cooperative swapping of skills and information. Write:

> Volunteer Readership
> Box 1807
> Boulder, CO 80306

Joan Flanagan. *The Grass Roots Fundraising Book*. This is a new book on local fund-raising for nonprofit groups. For ordering information write:

> 1981 Volunteer Readership Catalog
> Volunteer Readership
> Box 1807
> Boulder, CO 80306

People Power: What Communities are Doing to Counter Inflation. U.S. Office of Consumer Affairs. Success stories featuring self-help group projects of diverse sorts. Free. Write:

> *People Power*
> Consumer Information Center
> Dept. 682-H
> Pueblo, CO 81009

General and Profit Barter Publications

Dyanne Asimow Simon. *The Barter Book: The Consumer's Guide to Living Well Without Using Money*. E.P. Dutton, NY, 1979. An excellent book on barter as alternative economics, with much practical advice and a bibliography. Unfortunately, many of the independent barter groups listed in the Appendix no longer exist.

Charles Morrow Wilson. *Let's Try Barter: The Answer to Inflation (and the Tax Collector)*. NY, 1960, 1980. Long out of print but recently re-issued, this is a very readable barter classic full of common sense and true barter stories, many from Wilson's bartering childhood at Bill Plue's general store in Mount Comfort, Arkansas.

Constance Stapleton and Phyllis C. Richman. *Barter: How to Get Almost Anything Without Money*. NY, 1978. Lots of good ideas for new barterers.

David W. London, ed. *How to Barter*. Walnut Creek, CA, 1980. Published by the Comstock Trading Post, a barter club, this small book contains several essays on sophisticated bartering techniques for experienced swappers. The Appendix has the most up-to-date listing of exchange groups in print.

George W. Burtt. *The Barter Way to Beat Inflation*. NY, 1980. Strictly for profit barterers; a vigorous, wheeler-dealer approach.

Barter Communique. Box 2527, Sarasota, FL 33578. Sample copy, $5. The publication of a firm of professional reciprocal traders that lists all sorts of business exchange possibilities.

Al Lowry. *How You Can Become Financially Independent by Investing in Real Estate*. For ordering information, write:

Nickerson Educational Advancement Institute
50 Washington Street
Reno, NV 89503

Advice by a professional real estate investor who also conducts weekend seminars on the same subject. Very similar is the series of books on real estate trading by Robert W. Steele, available from:

>   Newport Book and Seminar Company
>   Box 1554
>   Medford, OR 97501

There are literally hundreds of real estate barter organizations, both loose and informal, all over the country. Dave London's *How to Barter* (see above) lists more than 150 of them.

As we've seen, one of the basic techniques in real estate trading is to get an undervalued property, improve it, and swap "up" for another. The same technique can be applied to rural real estate, whether raw land, a rundown farm, or an old house on a few acres. Here are a few publications of interest to rural swappers.

Jean Young and Jim Young. *Buying Right in Country Real Estate*. New York: New American Library, 1979.

The Old-House Journal is a monthly newsletter dealing with the solutions to renovation and repair problems in old houses. $16 a year. Write:

>   *The Old-House Journal*
>   69A Seventh Avenue
>   Brooklyn, NY 11217

The same organization has put out a manual for restoring pre-1920 houses called *The Old-House Journal Compendium,* at $19.95, The Overlook Press, Woodstock, NY.

Smalltown, USA is a unique newsletter reporting on small towns all across the country. Order from Woods Creek Press, Box 339, Ridgecrest, CA 93555. To save you the tedious problem of tracking down newell posts, door knobs, spiral staircase builders, copper-roofing experts, and manufacturers of hundreds of items for restoring old houses, see: Lawrence Grow, ed. *Old House Catalog*. Warner Books, NY, $9.95.

Trade Clubs

Business Exchange, Inc. (BX)
4716 Vineland Avenue
North Hollywood, CA 91602

Membership $195, with $36 annual dues. Eight percent cash charge on purchases. Computer, barter checkbook, directory. Offices in the following cities:

Mobile, Alabama	Des Moines, Iowa
Scottsdale, Arizona	Bangor, Maine
Alhambra, California	New Castle, New
Bellflower, California	Hampshire
Fremont, California	Portsmouth, New
Goleta, California	Hampshire
Joshua Tree, California	Ridgewood, New Jersey
Los Angeles, California	Albuquerque, New Mexico
Oxnard, California	Hamburg, New York
San Diego, California	Kernersville, North
Santa Ana, California	Carolina
Ottawa, Ontario, Canada	Oklahoma City, Oklahoma
Toronto, Ontario, Canada	Portland, Oregon
Jacksonville, Florida	Knoxville, Tennessee
Atlanta, Georgia	Dallas, Texas
Coeur d'Alene, Idaho	Longview, Texas
Rockford, Illinois	Salt Lake City, Utah
Indianapolis, Indiana	Seattle, Washington

Exchange Enterprises
159 West Haven Avenue
Salt Lake City, UT 84115

Membership $25, $175 annual dues in advance. Ten percent charge on purchases. Member I.D. cards. No directory. Liaison with fellow swappers through central office. Offices in the following cities:

Anchorage, Alaska	Twin Falls, Idaho
Tempe, Arizona	Bettendorf, Iowa
Melbourne, Australia	Missoula, Montana
Costa Mesa, California	Omaha, Nebraska
Garden Grove, California	Las Vegas, Nevada
Lafayette, California	Reno, Nevada
LaMesa, California	Columbus, Ohio
Sacramento, California	Oklahoma City, Oklahoma
San Jose, California	Portland, Oregon
Stockton, California	Dallas, Texas
Wheatridge, Colorado	Houston, Texas
Honolulu, Hawaii	Bellevue, Washington
Idaho Falls, Idaho	Spokane, Washington
Meridian, Idaho	Tacoma, Washington

Mutual Credit
6300 Variel Street
Woodland Hills, CA 91367

Deposit of $300 (credited to member's account in trade dollars). Eight percent fee on purchases, 5 percent on sales. Fees may be automatically deducted from member's bank account or debited to major charge cards. Other electronic accounting procedures available. Offices in the following cities:

Anchorage, Alaska	Campbell, California
Phoenix, Arizona	Concord, California
Tucson, Arizona	Foster City, California

Fresno, California
Garden Grove, California
Novato, California
Oxnard, California
Riverside, California
Sacramento, California
San Mateo, California
Santa Rosa, California
Tahoe City, California
Vallejo, California
Venice, California
Surrey, British Columbia,
    Canada
Waterloo, Ontario, Canada
Arvada, Colorado
Colorado Springs,
    Colorado
Denver, Colorado
Fort Collins, Colorado
Northglenn, Colorado
Westminster, Colorado
Casselberry, Florida
Fort Lauderdale, Florida
Jacksonville, Florida
Lakeland, Florida
Maitland, Florida
Merritt Island, Florida
Orlando, Florida
St. Petersburg, Florida
Atlanta, Georgia
Honolulu, Hawaii
Lahaina, Maui, Hawaii
Boise, Idaho
Hesston, Kansas
Wichita, Kansas
St. Paul, Minnesota
Carson City, Nevada
Las Vegas, Nevada
Reno, Nevada

Hazlet, New Jersey
Newark, New Jersey
Buffalo, New York
Niagara Falls, New York
Edmund, Oklahoma
Tulsa, Oklahoma
Ashland, Oregon
Coos Bay, Oregon
Corvallis, Oregon
Medford, Oregon
Newport, Oregon
Pendleton, Oregon
Portland, Oregon
Roseburg, Oregon
Salem, Oregon
Sherwood, Oregon
Springfield, Oregon
Charlotte, South Carolina
Greenville, South Carolina
Myrtle Beach, South
    Carolina
Germantown, Tennessee
Memphis, Tennessee
Dallas, Texas
El Paso, Texas
Odessa, Texas
San Antonio, Texas
Salt Lake City, Utah
Bellingham, Washington
Centralia, Washington
Everett, Washington
Federal Way, Washington
Longview, Washington
Mount Vernon, Washington
Seattle, Washington
Spokane, Washington
Tacoma, Washington
Vancouver, Washington
Milwaukee, Wisconsin

International Trade Exchange
7656 Burford Drive
McLean, VA 22101

Headquarters for franchised clubs. Average franchise about $20,000. Local club membership $150 to $200 plus. Another $100 allows trading privileges with other ITE clubs. Ten percent trade fees. Affiliates in the following cities:

Little Rock, Arkansas	East Brunswick, New
Danbury, Connecticut	Jersey
East Hartford, Connecticut	Albany, New York
Altamonte Springs, Florida	Rochester, New York
Fort Lauderdale, Florida	Tonawanda, New York
Jacksonville, Florida	Hickory, North Carolina
Pensacola, Florida	Cincinnati, Ohio
Atlanta, Georgia	Dayton, Ohio
Chicago, Illinois	Perrysburg, Ohio
Rockford, Illinois	Youngstown, Ohio
Indianapolis, Indiana	Harrisburg, Pennsylvania
Des Moines, Iowa	King of Prussia,
Valley Center, Kansas	Pennsylvania
Versailles, Kentucky	West Chester, Pennsylvania
Lake Charles, Louisiana	Columbia, South Carolina
Shreveport, Louisiana	Brentwood, Tennessee
Portland, Maine	Sweetwater, Tennessee
Worcester, Massachusetts	Amarillo, Texas
Warren, Michigan	Dallas, Texas
Jackson, Minnesota	El Paso, Texas
Auburn, New Hampshire	Lubbock, Texas
Burlington, New Jersey	San Antonio, Texas
	Virginia Beach, Virginia

There are many independent trade clubs scattered all over the country, some with only 100 members, others with more than 1,000. Some of them specialize in goods, some in services, some in information and instruction like the well-known Learning Exchange in Evanston, Illinois. Similar are the Learning Community in Portland, Oregon, and Free-For-All in Los Angeles, California. These organizations are braintrusts of experts in hundreds of fields from psychology to stellar navigation. In the same category is Swap-A-Skill at San Jose State University in California, where skills and information are traded. This is a student movement of swapped tutorials.

Seeds

If you are interested in gardening—and what rural swapper isn't—keep your eyes open for seed exchanges. Some seed companies will swap for your special heirloom varieties. One has made a seed-swap business of it.

> The True Seed Exchange
> Kent Whealy
> RR #2
> Princeton, MO 64673

The True Seed Exchange specializes in heirloom and traditional old strains of seed no longer available through regular markets.

Swap Columns

Several magazines and papers offer space for swaps. Two of the best known are *Yankee,* Dublin, NH 03444 and *Mother Earth News,* Box 70, Hendersonville, NC 28739. Check the classified ad section of your favorite magazines. Often there are swap offers.

House Swapping

If you are interested in swapping your house for a few weeks or longer with someone for a free vacation, here are some of the leading house-swapping organizations. In addition, many barter club members swap vacation houses through the club.

Vacation Exchange Club
350 Broadway
New York, NY 10013

Forty-five hundred listings and a circulation of 10,000. Many foreign listings. Subscription, $12.

Inquiline, Inc.
35 Adams Street
Bedford Hills, NY 10507

Eight-hundred-member listing, many foreign. 2,000 subscribers. Fee: $35, includes annual directory, quarterly newsletters, and a booklet on vacation houses for rent. Subscription plus listing is $50.

Holiday Exchanges
Box 878
Belen, NM 87002

Five hundred subscribers and listings, mostly all United States. $15 for a year's subscription of the monthly directory and a one-time listing.

InterService Home Exchange
Box 87
Glen Echo, MD 20768

Two hundred subscribers and listings, some foreign. $15 for five bulletins a year plus a listing in the annual directory.

Adventures in Living
Box 278
Winnetka, IL 60093

Five hundred listings and many more subscribers. About one-third of the listings from fourteen foreign countries. $25 for a small handbook on house exchanging, a listing in the annual directory, and two supplements.

INDEX